The Parent's Guide to HORSEBACK RIDING

JESSICA JAHIEL, Ph.D.

ROXBURY PARK

LOWELL HOUSE
LOS ANGELES
NTC/Contemporary Publishing Group

Library of Congress Cataloging-in-Publication Data

Jahiel, Jessica.
    The parent's guide to horseback riding / by Jessica Jahiel.
       p.   cm.
    Includes bibliographical references and index.
    ISBN 0-7373-0040-X
    1. Horses. 2. Horsemanship. 3. Children and animals. I. Title.
SF285.J35 1999
798.2'3—dc21
                                         99-18259
                                           CIP

Published by Lowell House
A division of NTC/Contemporary Publishing Group, Inc.
4255 West Touhy Avenue, Lincolnwood (Chicago), Illinois 60646-1975 U.S.A.

© 1999 by Jessica Jahiel
Cover photograph copyright © 1997 Bill Ling/Telegraph Colour Library/FPG International LLC.

Lowell House books can be purchased at special discounts when ordered in bulk for premiums and special sales. Contact Department CS at the following address:

NTC/Contemporary Publishing Group
4255 West Touhy Avenue
Lincolnwood, IL 60646-1975
1-800-323-4900

Roxbury Park is a division of
NTC/Contemporary Publishing Group, Inc.

Managing Director and Publisher: Jack Artenstein
Editor in Chief, Roxbury Park Books: Michael Artenstein
Director of Publishing Services: Rena Copperman
Editorial Assistant: Nicole Monastirsky
Interior Illustrator: Clara Lawrence

Printed and bound in the United States of America
10 9 8 7 6 5 4 3 2 1

To all non-horsey parents who are bemused
by their children's inexplicable passion for horses.

CONTENTS

Acknowledgments

To Charlotte Kneeland, who created the American Riding Instructor Certification Program (ARICP). And to my friends and colleagues at ARICP who share their expertise, ethics, and energy with their students through their teaching and their time with so many riding instructors every November at the ARICP National Seminar.

Bob Allen, Denny Emerson, Susan Harris, George Morris, and Sally Swift—I am constantly inspired by all of you. I'm proud to have you as colleagues; I'm honored to have you as friends.

INTRODUCTION

There are hundreds—thousands—of books that can help readers learn how to ride or how to ride better. This isn't one of them. It won't explain how to ride or what forms of riding your children might enjoy—many books already do these things very well. Your children probably already own several such books. This isn't a book for your children; it's a book for you: a guide for parents who may not have any experience with horses, but whose children are determined to learn to ride and eventually to have horses of their own.

Parents in your situation can feel confused, lost, and alone. Since the focus of your efforts is entirely on your children, your children's riding, and the horses that your children ride under the direction of other adults, parents in your situation can also feel unimportant and forgotten. In fact, you are neither: It's only your support and encouragement that allows your children to experience the joy of riding, and no matter how oblivious they may seem, somewhere at the back of their minds, your children know this and appreciate what you do for them.

I hope that this book will help you find your way through some of the less-commonly explored areas of the horse world and that it will allow you to realize you are neither lost nor alone. Your parenting skills and good sense are more useful than you know, and you are never far from help or advice. This book offers you both: direct advice about children, horses, expenses, and safety, and access to a wealth of resources; videotapes, books, Web sites, and telephone numbers.

Nothing is more important to you than the safety and happiness of your children. Since you are reading this, it's obvious that you know, or are beginning to know, that nothing is more important to your children than horses. Their interest may flare only briefly or it may be the start of a lifelong passion. In either case, you need to be well armed with information that will help you find the instructor, the stable, the horse, and the equipment to minimize the risks and maximize the athletic, mental, and emotional benefit, as well as the pure enjoyment that riding can bring your child.

DR. JESSICA JAHIEL

CHAPTER 1
Children and Horses

If you live in the country and have always had horses, you may have a horse-crazy child. If you live in the suburbs, own a dog or a cat, and see horses only through the car windows on your way into the city, you may have a horse-crazy child. If you live in the city, in an apartment, you have never taken your child to see a horse, and your landlord's idea of an acceptable pet is a goldfish, you may still have a horse-crazy child.

WHY IS MY CHILD HORSE-CRAZY?

Children are naturally attracted to horses, and children have a knack for finding out about horses and falling in love with them. They don't need to be in the presence of a real horse for the magic to occur.

Falling in Love with Horses

Your child may fall in love with horses at summer camp, or after visiting a friend who owns a horse, or after taking one lesson at the local riding stable. Or your child may fall in love with horses even though she has never been near a horse. Posters, pictures, magazines, model horses, sweaters, and shirts with horse images on them are popular with children of all ages.

How It Starts Be prepared. That innocent hayride for the fourth-grade class, a glimpse of a rider on the trail or the beach during your family vacation—even the carousel at the fair can be the trigger for a temporary or permanent addiction to horses. It can be a lifelong condition, and in most cases there is no cure. Fortunately, no cure is needed! Horses are good for children, provided that the children are taught to ride them well, handle them correctly, and deal with them honestly and kindly. That's where the parents come in. Properly approached, an addiction to horses will improve your child in every way: physically, mentally, and emotionally.

What You Can Do Does your child adore horses? If you don't know anything about horses, or if you know just enough to feel that they are large and expensive, you need to read this book carefully, because you are going to have horses in your life. Never underestimate

BOOKS

Usborne Guide to Riding and Pony Care

If your children are in the younger set—say ten and under—or if you yourself would like to begin with a very simple, basic book, this is a good one. This illustrated guide for children offers basic information on horses and riding. It provides definitions of common words and expressions and would be suitable for parents who are new to the horse world.

the initiative, drive, determination, creativity, and sheer persistence of horse-crazy children. If your child is consumed by the love of horses, you are going to enter the world of horses somehow, somewhere, whether you want to or not. As an adult, you know better than to leap into any venture without sufficient information. Your responsibility as a parent will compel you to do homework on the subject, and that is what you are doing right now.

Horses and children; children and horses. Whether your child enjoys riding for the physical pleasure of it, or for the communication with a member of another species, or has dreams of the Olympics, the connection and the benefits are very real. Competitions aren't necessary; large ambitions aren't required. Riding is a wonderful sport regardless of the individual rider's goals and level of ambition.

The horse-crazy child will find horses somewhere.

Is Riding Expensive? Yes, it's an expensive sport—but no more so than many others. Parents who routinely pay for tennis or golf lessons, or who hire a skating coach and pay for ice time, know what sort of financial commitment is involved in almost any sport.

ARE HORSES GOOD FOR CHILDREN?

Horses can be the best thing that ever happened to children. Children can derive many benefits from riding and caring about horses. Physical development is just one benefit. Like ballet and the martial arts, riding requires balance, coordination, body awareness, and body control. Like swimming, running, or bicycling, riding promotes even, bilateral physical development. And as with all of these disciplines, the benefits of riding come to all who participate. It isn't necessary for your child to win competitions, or even to compete at all, in order to derive all the physical benefits that riding can offer.

Emotional Benefits of Riding

Your child's emotional and mental development will also benefit from association with horses—and so will your child's character. To become a good rider, your child will need to learn to be calm, patient, generous, and kind. In addition to these qualities and the physical benefits, riding also requires and develops two all-important attributes: responsibility and accountability.

Learning Responsibility By learning to look after horses, children learn to take responsibility for the well-being of another living entity that is entirely dependent on them. Pony Club instructors have long observed that Pony Clubbers grow up to become excellent parents; throughout their years in Pony Club, they learn and are reminded that the interests of the horse must come before their own, that the horse must be well looked after and treated with kindness and understanding, that it must be fed appropriately and given regular medical attention, that the horse is dependent on its owner/rider, and that the rider's first responsibility is always to the horse. This understanding, these skills, and the habits created during these years carry over easily to adulthood and parenthood.

Competition Can Be Useful In the proper setting—one in which horsemanship and sportsmanship are paramount—competition can be a good thing. Through competition, children can learn to be gracious when they win—and when they don't. They can learn to take the ribbons and the disappointments in stride.

What Are Your Values? Competition also teaches children, very quickly, about the true values of their instructors and parents, so be aware that your reactions will be observed and noted and that your child will draw conclusions from them.

Q & A

Q: *My seven-year-old son is unfocused and silly when he plays at home, but at the barn he's a different child, a real "take-charge" type who suddenly reminds me of his daddy. What is it about horses that makes children change like this?*

A: I don't think your son is changing; I think that the horses bring out something that's there all the time but not necessarily visible.

Riding has a lot of appeal for children because it involves all of their senses at once. Since the horse reacts to them and they react to it, they tend to stay focused.

Riding is also very appealing because it puts the child in charge of the horse. For a small child, being in charge of a huge animal is truly exhilarating. Your son tells the horse to go this way or that, speed up, slow down, and stop—and the horse obeys. It can be hard for adults to remember what it felt like to be a child—we look back and think about freedom and fun. But there was a downside, too: Someone else was in control all the time. At the barn, on a horse, the instructor may be the one giving the directions, but the child is in direct charge of a thousand pounds of horse. It's a feeling that can't really be duplicated at home or at school.

Q: *My son is twelve, and I'm worried about him. He's been taking riding lessons for almost three years and until now seemed to be enjoying them very much. I've noticed lately that he doesn't spend much time at the barn anymore, and when I take him to his lessons he comes out right afterward instead of making me come in and find him after half an hour.*

It's a nice barn and the instructor is very good, and good with kids. I haven't wanted to mention this to her in case she thought I was criticizing her teaching, but for the last few weeks, Ryan has missed lessons because he had extra homework or a stomachache. Today he said that lessons were boring, and I know that's not true.

He's in a class of five riders, and the other four are girls. This never bothered him before, but now it seems to bother him a lot. Maybe talking to his instructor would help, I don't know. I'm going to have to do it if the situation doesn't improve. I'm very disappointed because Ryan is still rather young and small for his age, and riding was a good sport for him, not like football or soccer.

A: Ryan is twelve, small and slight, obviously prepubescent, and sharing his riding lesson with girls of the same age. This is hard for boys, for several reasons. In Pony Club, there's a noticeable attrition around this time. If it's any comfort to you, I can tell you that many of the youngsters who loved riding when they were small but dropped out of the sport when they were Ryan's age eventually came back to it.

Girls and boys don't mature at the same rate, and at this time in Ryan's life, the girls in his riding class are probably bigger, stronger, and better riders than he is. This is hard for boys to take—they believe, and are taught by their culture, that boys should be bigger, stronger, and faster than girls.

A child who claims a stomachache when it's time for a lesson is a child who doesn't want to be in that lesson. Talk to Ryan's instructor and see whether the two of you can't find a way to let him drop out for a while if that's what he wants. The instructor has probably seen this before.

In a few years, Ryan will be physically mature, and if he's still interested in riding, he'll probably choose to go back to it. If he doesn't, don't push him. He may also develop other interests, including some of those sports that weren't previously as appealing to him as was riding.

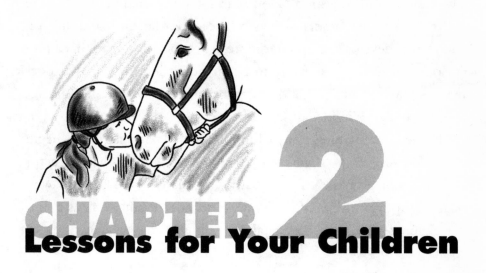

CHAPTER 2
Lessons for Your Children

If your child adores horses and has sufficient size, balance, and comprehension and a long-enough attention span to be safe in lessons, then you may begin looking for a riding instructor.

DON'T START TOO YOUNG

Everyone has heard anecdotes about toddlers who "started riding at three" or "rode at two"—take them with a grain of salt. At those ages, children aren't ready to sit on a pony safely unless someone else is holding them. Basket saddles for babies and leadline classes for toddlers have much more to do with parents' egos than with children's enjoyment of horses and riding.

Where to Begin

The answer to the question "How old should my child be?" is that age matters, but other factors such as balance, coordination, and physical and mental development matter more. This does not mean that a precocious four-year-old is ready to begin riding lessons. What it does mean is that a small and not quite coordinated child of eight is not yet ready to begin riding lessons.

In the United States Pony Clubs, we've had a few members begin at age five or even younger, but this is challenging for the instructor and does not give the child any advantage later on. The child who begins at four or five is often, at age nine, at the same level as a similar child of nine who began taking riding lessons at age seven or eight.

Small Children and Riding Not only are there often no advantages to a premature start, there are some clear disadvantages. If you look at the proportions of babies, children, and adults, you'll notice that the head reaches a large size quite early and that the body takes many more years to catch up. This is normal development that has certain implications for riding.

Very young children are less strong and coordinated than they will be in a few years; they are also top-heavy. An adult sitting on a horse will notice that looking down to one side or the other can cause the rider's entire body to shift position, and if the horse makes a sudden movement while the rider is thus unbalanced, a fall can easily occur.

A very young child who looks down to one side or the other is almost guaranteed to fall, because the effort of rebalancing the little body under the heavy, unbalanced head and of rebalancing while on the horse is greater than most small children can manage. Add to this the difficulty in finding safety helmets to fit a very small child with a small head circumference and very little chin, and what you have is not a young rider getting an early start, but an accident in the making.

Balance and body proportions aren't the only age-related issues. There are other considerations that will affect your decision about when to start your child in riding lessons: attention span, sustainable energy level, physical strength, and coordination. Beyond the physical considerations, there are emotional and mental ones that will also affect the child's comfort and safety; these include level of emotional security, grasp of concepts, and vocabulary.

What Are Age-Appropriate Lessons?

Lessons, especially during the first few months, will not consist of a full hour in the saddle. A very young child will spend proportionately less time in the saddle than an older child. Children of five, six, and seven can benefit from time spent with horses, and they can enjoy simple,

Learning the parts of the horse's body.

age-appropriate unmounted lessons and occasional "pony rides" with an adult walking alongside.

First Steps Early lessons for children ages eight to ten should be brief and should be taught on small, gentle, child-tolerant horses and ponies. There should be constant direct supervision by the instructor, who should be dealing with no more than one to four children. The lessons themselves should provide a little time in the saddle, perhaps at a standstill, doing exercises, and a lot of time learning to brush and halter and lead the horse, clean the horse's feet, and identify parts of the horse and tack.

Tacking Up Don't be surprised if your child has to reach a certain age and size and earn the "right" to tack up a horse. Some instructors encourage riders to take responsibility for tacking up from the very beginning; others prefer to do it themselves for the first few weeks while the students watch so that the tack is always put on correctly and gently.

When the students understand how to tack up, they begin to do it themselves under the instructor's supervision; finally, when they have proven themselves competent, they will be allowed to do it on their own. This avoids the problems that can be seen at too many stables: horses that have become headshy after being forcibly bridled by too many inept riders; and horses that become "girthy" or develop sores from an improperly adjusted saddle and pad or an incorrectly tightened girth.

The instructor's liability may also be a factor in this caution. A horse in pain from ill-fitting or poorly adjusted equipment is much less safe than a horse wearing comfortable tack.

Grooming Riders can learn about grooming from the very first day at the barn, even if they are very young and the grooming consists of wiping a brush over the coat of a small pony while the instructor looks on. If your child spends time (one to three months) grooming the horse and then observes while the instructor tacks it up, this is good. When children are ready to tack up the horse under supervision and eventually by themselves, they'll be ready and will do it right.

HOW DO WE BEGIN?

If there is a Pony Club in your area, talk to the DC (short for "District Commissioner"—the individual in charge of a particular club). Pony Club is dedicated to teaching children up to the age of twenty-one all about riding and horsemanship, and your child won't need a horse to join. Pony Club provides mounted and unmounted meetings, lessons, lectures, clinics, field trips, and competitions.

Pony Clubbers may use one another's horses with permission; sometimes the DC or the instructor has school horses or horses to lend. Pony Club parents are usually very generous about helping other Pony Clubbers get to meetings—you'll probably be able to carpool for unmounted meetings and trailer pool for mounted meetings.

Pony Club gives children the chance to acquire an equestrian education and learn to improve their riding, horse care, and social skills, including the ability to work effectively within peer groups. It teaches them responsibility and accountability in an atmosphere of activity and fun. It allows them to set and meet goals, and—very important for children and adults alike—it allows them to do all of this in an environment where the standards are specific and clear, and where effort and achievements are recognized and rewarded.

Pony Club also offers a great advantage to parents, in that the standards are clearly described in the Pony Club Manuals of Horsemanship as well as in other publications available to Pony Clubbers and their parents. Armed with this sort of comprehensive information, you will be much better equipped to evaluate stables, instructors, horse care, and the level of your child's continuing interest.

HORSES AND YOUR HANDICAPPED CHILD

If your child is handicapped and addicted to horses, congratulations— riding is a wonderful developmental exercise for the handicapped child. Even for children who can do no more than sit passively as the horse carries them at a walk, the benefits will be enormous.

The movements of the horse underneath the rider's body imitate the walking movements that humans make; the joints and muscles of your child's body are stimulated in the same way that they would be if your child were walking unaided. The height, the freedom of movement, the temporary possession of legs that work perfectly—all of these serve to strengthen the handicapped child's body and spirit. And a horse makes an excellent friend and confidant, guaranteed never to reveal the secrets of any child.

Hippotherapy, recreational riding, and remedial vaulting—a sort of gymnastics on horseback—can all be of immense benefit to the handicapped child.

What if the handicap isn't physical? The quality of the experience will depend to a great extent on the capabilities of the instructor, but this is true for all children who learn to ride. For riders who are slow to comprehend but physically secure and able, riding a horse is an accessible skill that may allow them to shine. Don't underrate your child: There's a way for most people to enjoy horses and riding, regardless of their physical or mental capacity. There are stables that specifically cater to handicapped riders; there are catalogues of equipment made specifically for riders with special needs.

For a handicapped rider, "shine" doesn't mean only in the confines of a particular lesson facility. There are competition venues for handicapped riders, up to and including the international level at the Paralympics. It's impressive and moving to see the effort and commitment of these riders and of the people who have helped them reach for their dreams.

RESOURCES

For Handicapped Riders

North American Riding for the Handicapped Association (NARHA)
P.O. Box 33150
Denver, CO 80233
1-800-369-RIDE

Freedom Rider (for the challenged equestrian)
info@freedomrider.com
1-888-253-8811

Riding for the Disabled by Vanessa Britton

Q & A

Q: My daughter wants to jump, but that seems dangerous to me. Isn't she more likely to get hurt if she's taking jumping lessons?

A: Not really. If you find a good instructor who will allow her to learn at her own pace so that her confidence and understanding develop along with her physical skills, jumping will be one more way to have fun riding.

The research done by the American Medical Equestrian Association and other groups has indicated, over and over, that most riding accidents and injuries occur *not* over jumps but on the flat, and not at a gallop but at a walk or a standstill.

The only way you can know that your daughter will never be injured falling from a horse is if you undertake to keep her off horses forever—and that's not a very good choice. It's better to allow her to take lessons, including jumping lessons, with a good instructor who won't rush things and who will teach your daughter not only good riding skills but good safety habits.

Q: *My husband and I bought a horse for our daughter, and right now it's about the only thing she cares about. She's rude and obnoxious at home, and she doesn't care if I take away her allowance. She would care if I kept her at home and didn't let her go to the barn, but she knows I won't punish her by keeping her away from the barn. I know that the horse needs its regular care and exercise and stall cleaning, so I take her to the barn every day even if I'm furious with her. I've been thinking that perhaps I could punish her by taking away her lessons whenever she's been really bad. That way, she would suffer but the horse wouldn't. What do you think?*

A: I think it's a bad idea. If the horse were a car, would you take away her driving privileges or would you take away her Driver Education lessons? She needs those lessons—and the horse needs her to have those lessons. The better rider she becomes, the more comfortable the horse will be.

If you really need to deprive your daughter of something to do with horses, don't take away her lessons. Instead, why not keep her at home, away from the barn and her daily time with her horse? Or take her allowance to pay someone else at the barn to clean her horse's stall and turn her horse out for exercise? That way, the horse won't suffer, but you'll have managed to get your daughter's attention.

Some counseling might be a good idea. This kind of behavior sounds as if it's a bit beyond that of a normal kid having a bad day, and if there's a problem in some part of your daughter's life, you need to know about it and do something about it as soon as you possibly can.

Q: My son has cerebral palsy and is definitely a "special needs" child. I had such fun riding when I was small, I'd really like him to enjoy the same pleasure. But I'm not sure that he could handle it, and I wouldn't want to set him up to fail. He gets very excited and happy whenever he sees a horse so I think he would like to try riding if he could do it.

A: There may be a therapeutic riding center near you. Find out by calling the North American Riding for the Handicapped Association at 1-800-369-RIDE. Assisted riding could be difficult and complex for you and is not something you should attempt on your own. But for the trained staff at therapeutic riding centers, it's all in a day's work. The concept of "failure" doesn't come into it—contact the NARHA, find a center, and give it a try.

Q: My little nine-year-old granddaughter just adores horses, and I've been thinking about buying her one as a surprise for her birthday. I can afford to pay for its upkeep if her parents aren't willing to do that, so I don't think this would create a problem. Any suggestions?

A: Certainly—don't do it! Not as a surprise, anyway. It's okay to surprise the child, but if you surprise her parents, it may be a long time before all of you are on speaking terms again. Her parents have to be involved in this from the very beginning, even if the horse is a gift from you and even if you are going to pay for the board.

I have a better suggestion: Talk to her parents and tell them that you would like to give your granddaughter riding lessons with a certified instructor for her birthday. A year's worth of riding lessons and her riding clothes would be a much more appropriate present than a horse.

Look at it this way: Many children "just adore" horses but don't really enjoy riding them; some enjoy riding horses but don't really want to have the work of owning and looking after one. Your granddaughter is young, and until she's had the chance to learn to ride, neither you, she, nor her parents will know what she really wants.

Give her the lessons—you'll be giving her a very meaning-ful gift. And if she proves to be a wonderful rider and horse-woman who truly wants and deserves to own a horse, she'll have another birthday every year. There's time. I understand that you want to see her enjoying her own horse now, and that it would give you pleasure to provide that horse, but she'll appreciate and enjoy it much more in a year or two, so be patient, and in the meantime, enjoy her enjoyment of the lessons you're going to give her.

Q: *I've visited two different riding academies in my area, but I don't know which one to choose. I'm leaning toward one because the instruc-tor seems more professional. She was willing to tell me when my chil-dren would be ready to canter and jump. The other place is also very nice, but the instructor there would not give me any information about what the children would be able to do in two, four, and six months. All she would tell me is "Most of our riders learn to canter and jump small jumps by the end of the first year." Wouldn't this mean that the first academy is superior? They certainly seem to teach faster.*

A: All other things (facilities, horses, tack, etc.) being equal, I would choose the second riding school. "How long will it take my child to learn to canter?" is a question that's impossible to answer definitively. Learning to ride is a process of acquiring skills, and the point of riding lessons is to help children acquire those skills. Children differ in their ability, in their interest, in the speed with which they acquire different skills, and in the speed at which they can process new material comfortably. If you have two children, you may find that even at the same barn with the same instructor, one learns certain skills faster than the other. It's an individual matter, and the ideal riding instructor will help each child acquire each new skill and only then move on.

It's not realistic, professional, or even ethical for an instructor to promise that a student will be cantering in five weeks or jumping in five months. An exceptionally strong, supple, coordinated child may indeed be cantering in five weeks or even sooner. A timid and not very coordinated child may just be mastering the posting trot after eight or ten weeks.

Different children will take different amounts of time to acquire a given skill or set of skills. It would be wrong to hold a child back if she is ready to canter after only four weeks; it would be even more wrong to push slower children into doing something beyond their current ability, in order to meet parents' expectations or an arbitrary schedule.

Another issue is that of individual versus group lessons. It's best for the child if the first lessons are one-on-one; in the beginning, any beginning rider needs the instructor's complete attention. Group lessons are wonderful for children who have acquired a good base set of skills; at that point, the riders can benefit from watching one another. There is more profit to be made from teaching group lessons, so you may have to look hard and pay more to get individual instruction for a child, but for the first year (at least) it's worth it.

Finding a Barn

CHAPTER 3

If your child is going to ride, you will need to compare and evaluate the suitability of various lesson barns. Don't allow your child to investigate and decide which stable is best; children often prefer to ride where their friends ride, and horse-crazy children will want to ride at the first place that has real, live horses available. Passion doesn't imply good judgment; you have to provide that yourself, using a combination of homework and common sense.

IS THIS THE RIGHT BARN?
HOW WILL I KNOW?

Your child's priority is HORSES. Your priorities are, in order: your child's safety; the quality of your child's equestrian education; and your ability to get your child to and from the stable at the appointed times regardless of weather or traffic conditions. The last is the easiest for you to evaluate: like homes, stables are often judged by three criteria—location, location, location.

Location Matters—What Else?

Although there is a good deal to be said for a stable with a convenient location, the people are more important than the facilities. "Fancy" isn't important, but "safe, clean, organized, and professional" very much are, and these are the qualities you need to identify. Go to the heart of the subject—don't be distracted by mahogany stalls or solid-brass nameplates. Look for a well-run, clean facility full of sound, happy (not necessarily beautiful) horses that aren't overworked. Look for tackrooms full of clean, well-maintained tack, simple snaffles, and clean saddlepads.

The best barn may not be the most expensive, successful, or profitable one; the things you want are good horse care, good instruction, and good rider progress, and those depend on the ethics and professionalism of the manager, instructor(s), and staff. These things matter even more than location—the barn nearest you may be the most convenient, but you need to know that your child will be safe during lessons and stay safe if you are delayed picking her up.

Visit barns, watch, listen, ask questions. Take notes in a notebook and pay attention to your gut feelings as well. Attend a few local shows and keep your eyes and ears open. If you see that horses and riders from one barn always look better, quieter, more proficient than the ones from other barns, ask to visit that barn and watch a few lessons. If you feel good about sending your child there, give it a try.

Of course it's helpful to be an experienced rider and horse handler, but if you aren't, that doesn't mean you are helpless or at the mercy of a fast talker with a barn full of lame school horses. You can read some general horse information books and horse care books, and you can talk to people you trust. Ask questions, learn what to look for—good and bad signs—and keep your eyes wide open all the time.

What Else Should I Look for?

Inspect the stables for cleanliness and organization, watch the instructor teach, look at the condition and quality of the schoolhorses and the tack. Watch how the students treat the horses, and notice how the instructor reacts—you'll figure out the instructor's philosophy and attitude very quickly.

If you visit a barn and have a bad feeling about the place, the instructor, the horses, or the other students, keep looking for the right place. Trust your instincts and common sense, do your homework on the subject.

You don't need to speak Spanish to know whether your child is learning and gaining skills and self-confidence in Spanish class; you don't need to speak Spanish to get a clear impression of the good (or not) qualities of the Spanish teacher. If your child and the other students

School horses should look calm and healthy, and wear simple, suitable tack.

are pleasant, cheerful, interested, and hardworking, and seem to handle the language easily and make themselves understood, you can probably safely assume that the teacher is a good one.

If the students are worried, resentful, bored, and incapable of communicating, you can probably assume that the teacher is a bad one. All of this is just as true for riding. You don't have to be a riding expert or a horse expert—you know how to observe behavior, demeanor, activity, and interest level, and you will draw the appropriate conclusions.

I THINK I'VE FOUND THE RIGHT BARN— NOW WHAT?

Talk to the stable manager, the riding instructor, and, if possible, to the staff. You will want to be on good terms with everyone. Read the boarding contract, lesson contract, or lease contract carefully before you sign, and ask for clarification on any confusing points. Ask to see the stable's insurance policy; the manager of any reputable stable will be happy to show you the current liability policy.

Exchange Information

Ask questions about supervision in and out of lessons, about staff on the ground, about open hours, and about emergency procedures.

Information to Leave Also leave your information at the stable. A good, well-run facility will require that you leave contact information. The staff will need to know how to reach you in case of an emergency, and that means leaving them a list of numbers: yours, your spouse's, work numbers, cell phone, and pager numbers.

Leave information about your child. Again, a well-run facility will ask that you provide information including the name of your child's doctor and hospital and the clinic number, blood type, and known allergies.

Information to Take Home Pick up information at the stable; get a copy of the barn rules and go over them with your child, because you are both going to need to know them.

Make Sure You Understand the Rules Talk to the stable manager if you have any questions after reading the rules. You must be clear about *your* part in this: Are parents allowed or encouraged to watch? How long before the lesson can you leave the child at the barn, and how long after the lesson must the child be picked up?

B O O K S

Equine Law & Horse Sense
by Julie I. Fershtman

Fershtman specializes in equine law and writes clearly and intelligently about matters that are likely to concern every rider or horse owner.

In a lawsuit-happy world, books like these can help you protect yourself in your various horse transactions by helping you avoid the misunderstandings and subsequent litigation that happen all too frequently in the equine industry.

Ask About Drop-Off and Pick-Up Times Children love to spend extra time with the horses and the other children, but not all stables encourage riders to arrive early and leave late. Some prefer that riders appear, take their lessons, and then disappear—you will need to know your stable's policy. A riding stable is not a babysitting service and should not be used as one.

Learn to Walk the Line As a parent encouraging your child in a new interest, you will need to walk a fine line between watching over your child and interfering with the process. You should be there as much as possible in the beginning; don't assume that your child's safety and equestrian education can be turned over to someone else and that you can go on your way. You'll need to pay attention and stay in touch.

Ask Your Child Questions Children aren't always very forthcoming about what they learn. Whether you're asking "How was your riding lesson?" or "How was your day in school?," the answer may be "Okay I guess" or "Fine," neither of which offers you any information whatsoever. In the case of your child's riding lessons, what you don't know may hurt your child. Good instruction is invaluable—poor instruction is worse than useless and can put your child at risk. Don't take any chances.

VISIT AND VERIFY

Whether your child takes weekly or daily lessons, be sure that you too are present at the barn from time to time. If your child chooses to help out at the barn in exchange for extra instruction, check now and then to be sure that the arrangement isn't one-sided. If possible, keep the riding on a cash basis, and don't let your child work for lessons unless you are quite sure of what is going on.

Maintain a record of hours worked compared to lessons given, otherwise you may find out after several months that your child is mucking out stalls every afternoon in exchange for an occasional pony ride on the periphery of the paying students' lessons. Ethical instructors won't allow this to happen—and ethical instructors will encourage you to visit, watch, and keep track of all transactions.

Get information about your child's instructor, lesson program, and classes—and the other children in those classes. This will help you determine whether lessons are too crowded (more than four students), and it will help you arrange a lesson carpool with some of the other parents.

Once you are entirely comfortable with the instructor and the lessons, it will be time for you to retire discreetly until after the lessons are over. Don't hang around and watch lessons if your child doesn't want you to, even if it's okay with the instructor. Take something to do; you'll be able to work in the lounge or in your car. It's much better to take a few files or a book along than to sit empty-handed and impatient for your child to finish the lesson.

HORSES AND FAMILY TOGETHERNESS

There's an old saying, "Families that play together stay together." When horses are involved, that's very true. Common goals, values, and standards of care can keep parents and children communicating no matter how divisive the circumstance.

I know a woman in her forties who is taking riding lessons—so is her ten-year-old daughter. The daughter and mother have very different lives and might not have much to talk about, but they have the horses and their lessons in common, and they talk about horses and riding every day. That lets them lead into other areas—the daily communication is there, and this mother would continue to take riding lessons even if she didn't love the horses, because those moments of closeness and communication with her daughter are golden. While they drive to the barn together and chat, there is no generation gap, no mother/daughter conflict, nothing except two horse-crazy riders talking about their favorite subject.

Q & A

Q: *I'm confused about the difference between two local barns. One is apparently a "training barn" and the other is a "boarding barn," but my daughter has classmates who board their horses and take lessons at both places. Is there a real difference? The other girls' parents aren't clear about this either.*

A: The answer is "Maybe." In theory, a training barn is a competition-oriented facility at which horses are trained for competition, and their owners are taught to ride them in shows. The horses at such a barn are, for the most part, bred and sold by the owner of the facility. The trainer/instructor is in charge, and no outside instructors are allowed to teach there.

A boarding barn (again, in theory) is a facility set up to accommodate the horses of individuals who can't or don't choose to keep their horses at home. At a boarding barn, there may be no official instructor; riders have private instructors, and some of the riders might even teach one another.

That's the theory. In practice, the lines are very blurred. Many facilities have a resident instructor who may not be certified or even qualified to teach. Many barn owners offer lessons, training, and boarding services; many boarding barns won't allow boarders to take lessons with anyone other than the resident instructor, who may be the owner or manager.

Add to this the fact that people often name their barns according to what sounds good to them, even if the words don't reflect the nature of that particular facility. Thus, a boarding barn might be called a "Barn," "Stable," or "Farm"—some owners like to use the plural "Stables" or "Farms," which implies that this facility is just one of many that they own. Others like posh-sounding terms such as "Equestrian Center."

Then there are the barns where a change in ownership has led to a name change for the facility, and those where the name has remained the same for many years but the clientele has changed. A newly purchased and renamed facility originally designed for Western riding may still feature the 10'-x-10' stalls and undersized riding arena that were perfectly appropriate when it was still called "Jim's Ranch House."

An "Equestrian Center" may be a huge facility with several arenas, several instructors, and all manner of amenities, or it may be a small boarding barn with no resident instructor. The word *farm* may invoke images of green fields and horses grazing, but the facility may have no pastures, no grazing, and a six-horse trailer that takes boarders' and students' horses to a new show every weekend.

The only way to know is to inspect each facility, talk to the owner, and look at the amenities and the details of the lesson or boarding contract. Don't make any assumptions based on the listing in the telephone book. Instead, make a list of the services and amenities you need, and take it along on your inspection tour.

Q: I found what I thought was the ideal barn for my daughter's horse, but I'm beginning to wonder. The basic board cost was lower than most of the other barns, and the facilities were very similar, so it seemed like a good deal. The problem is that every month I get the bill for the current month with the "extras" for last month, and sometimes the total is nearly double what I was informed the basic board would be. Apparently our horse needs extra grain and hay every day because he eats so much, extra shavings for his stall bedding because he pees so much, extra turnout time or he gets "crazy" and the staff can't manage him, and so on. By the time I pay for an extra $150 of stuff that he "needs" every month, I could have taken him another couple of miles to the place I liked best, a really fancy facility that I thought was too expensive. In my opinion, all of those extras are just part of basic board, and ought to be included in what we're already paying. What should I do?

A: This is why you need to get everything in writing from the very beginning so that you can estimate your expenses and make more accurate barn-to-barn comparisons. You've learned an important fact the hard way: "Basic board" means whatever the barn owner wants it to mean, and you can't afford to make assumptions about what ought to be included.

Any good boarding barn will be happy to provide you with a list of services and charges, and the boarding contract itself should include information about how much hay and grain, how many bags of shavings, and how many hours of daily turnout time are included in the board.

Extra services should include things like putting blankets and boots on and taking them off again, administering medications, giving baths, grooming, clipping, braiding, transportation to and from shows, and perhaps even holding horses for the farrier or the vet, although some barns may offer the horse-holding service as part of the basic boarding contract.

A close comparison may show you that one barn's basic board offers a great deal more than another's. If you believe that you are paying too much for what you are getting at this boarding barn, you may want to move to another. If you do decide to move, check the terms of the boarding contract and the details of the charges for extra services before you go. You don't want to be disappointed again, and that's always a possibility if you don't read the fine print first.

CHAPTER 4
Dressing for the Sport

The clothing question leads to many others: What does your child actually need? Where can you get it? Should you buy new? Can you buy used? The answers, fortunately, are simple.

WHAT DOES THE RIDER NEED?

Essential equipment for riders is all rather sensible. Like equipment for skiing or skating, horseback-riding equipment should provide safety, comfort, and health. Safety equipment and clothing will come before tack, as safety equipment is required any time a child is riding.

Helmets and Safety

The safety helmet is the single most important item in your child's riding wardrobe. That helmet must meet or exceed the current American Standards for Testing and Materials/Safety Equipment Institute (ASTM/SEI) safety standards for equestrian helmets, and it must be fitted properly and worn with the safety harness properly adjusted and fastened whenever your child is mounted, even "just for a minute," even on a friend's sleepy small pony in a soft grassy pasture. A good safety helmet is an investment in your child. Get the right helmet—no bicycle helmets, no riding hats that are "items of apparel only," nothing but an ASTM/SEI tested and approved protective helmet designed specifically for equestrians. You'll learn more about helmets later in this book.

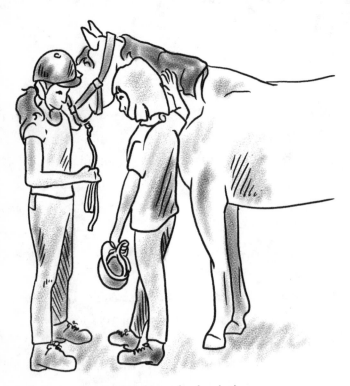

Casual clothes are fine for schooling.

Footgear and Safety

Boots are important to protect toes and ankles, but there is no need to purchase $600 custom leather tall boots for your young rider. For children, short boots designed for riding—paddock boots—are entirely appropriate, much less expensive, and much more practical.

When your child is older and is unlikely to change leg length or foot size, has become a proficient rider, and has expressed a strong desire to participate in more formal competitions, it will be time for you to begin to think about more formal, adult-style clothing.

Breeches

Breeches are practical. Jeans, unless designed specifically for riding and made from stretchy material, generally have seams in the most inconvenient places: in the crotch and inside the thighs. Riding pants—breeches, jodhpurs, and riding jeans—place the seams elsewhere so that they are not between the rider and saddle and so they don't cause chafing.

Breeches are meant to be worn with tall, knee-high riding boots; they are formfitting and fasten at the ankle with hook-and-loop fasteners or elastic; jodhpurs are meant to be worn with short, ankle-high riding boots, are a little longer, and generally end in cuffs. In practice, jodhpurs are generally more practical for children; if the child does wear tall boots, they generally fit quite nicely over the jodhpurs.

Breeches don't have to feature full leather seats; breeches don't have to be this month's popular color. Talk to the instructor about showing and schooling clothes.

Gloves

Gloves protect fingers, fingernails, and the skin between the fingers, and gloves make it easier for riders to hold the reins securely.

Q & A

Q: *My son is an eventer, and in the dressage test men are supposed to salute by removing their hats. This doesn't work if the "hat" is a safety helmet with a harness. Since this is the traditional way of doing things, should I just go ahead and let him wear an ordinary (non-protective) hunt cap for the dressage phase?*

A: No. He can wear his safety helmet for all three phases, and salute in an equally traditional way that is entirely acceptable for riders of both sexes. It's an easy method; when the rider halts, he should take both reins in his left hand and allow his right arm to drop, palm down, sweeping it back smoothly and slowly until it is held straight, just behind the thigh, palm facing rearward. At this point, the rider holds the arm in position for a moment and bows his head, then lifts his head and brings his right arm back into position, picks up the rein, and moves off.

The way to achieve a good salute is to do it smoothly and not too quickly. Sometimes it helps to practice it on a one-two-three count.

At the halt, sitting straight and looking straight ahead at the judge:

1. Take both reins in your left hand, and let your right arm fall slowly to your side.

Show clothing for young children and older children.

2. Bend your neck and lower your chin (the movement is really a slow, exaggerated nod, not a bow that involves your back) while continuing the movement of your right arm until the arm is straight and the hand is just behind your thigh.

3. Lift your chin and straighten your neck until you are looking straight ahead at the judge (who will nod or smile to acknowledge your salute); at the same time, bring your arm back up smoothly, pick up the reins, and prepare to move off.

A hurried salute makes a rider's movements look jerky and also gives the impression that the rider is worried that his horse will move off before he asks it to. If you make your one-two-three count a three-second count, the salute will be slow, graceful, and smooth.

Q: At my daughter's riding stable, all the kids in her group are around twelve years old. It's not a big show hunter barn, although some of the kids go to a few shows, but all the kids dress pretty much the same way: polo shirts and breeches. The problem is that Ellie is the only one who doesn't wear high riding boots, and it's starting to bother her.

I know that the books say jodhpurs and short boots are fine for kids, but Ellie isn't happy about it. She hasn't come right out and said that she wants high boots, but I know she does. Ellie is pretty good about not asking for things.

I'm a single mother, and we're on a budget, and Ellie's lessons are enough of an expense that I can't afford to do a lot of other fun things for her. And that includes high boots. I know that the good ones are several hundred dollars, and there's no way I can manage that kind of money.

Do you have any suggestions on how I can make Ellie feel better? I can't say a lot about the money situation because part of the problem is that her father has never paid one cent in child support since he left us four years ago, and she still loves her dad, and I don't want to ruin that feeling. I wish I could get the boots for her, though!

A: Ellie is very lucky to have you for a mother. It sounds to me as though she knows that. What I think is this: It would be great if Ellie could have a pair of tall boots, and perhaps I can offer some suggestions to make them more affordable. Brand new, good-quality boots are likely to be full price, but there are ways of finding used, good-quality boots for a much more reasonable price.

Visit every tack shop you can find, even the Western ones. Most tack shops have a consignment corner where local riders drop off their used equipment and clothing in the hope of making a little money from the sale of items they can no longer use. While you're at the tack shops, look in their new boots department—sometimes you'll find boots that were ordered by a customer who didn't like them or who never came back to get them. These boots are new but tend to sell for anywhere from a third to half off the retail price.

Visit every thrift shop you can find, and every resale boutique. I once found a lovely pair of boots for a student who was in a situation much like Ellie's—they fit perfectly, were in great shape, and we bought them at the Salvation Army store for $15. Those bargains don't come along every day, but it's always worth taking a look. Flea markets and garage sales can also be good sources of horse-related equipment and clothing.

Make a flyer that describes exactly what you're looking for: size, style, and condition. Be sure that you put in your contact information and mention that you're looking for "affordable used boots" so that you don't get calls from people with expensive boots for sale at high prices. Have your flyer copied onto colored paper (it attracts more attention) and put up copies everywhere horsey people are likely to go: tack shops, feed stores, and every boarding stable or riding stable in the area. If you can't drive everywhere, mail the flyers with notes asking stable owners to post them—they will.

Look for boots online. EBay (online auction) is a great place to shop—you might find the boots you want for a reasonable price. Don't limit yourself to leather boots. Cheap leather boots are worthless, as are cheap rubber boots, but there are good rubber boots that fit well, are comfortable, durable, not too hot, and are entirely suitable for showing. The best are made by Aigle. A pair of new Aigle Ecuyer boots (plain black dress-boot style) will cost $150 new but perhaps $75 or less if you can find a good used pair.

CHAPTER 5

Saddlery Comes Later

As long as your child is taking lessons on school horses, personal tack won't be needed. Personal equipment probably won't be required either, but all children want to have a personal grooming box, whether they have a horse to groom or not.

WHAT DO I NEED TO BUY?

That plastic tote packed with brushes and hoofpicks may not seem like much to you, but it means a great deal to your child—it's proof of association with horses, and psychologically is one step closer to horse ownership. Later, if you lease a horse, your child will undoubtedly want personal buckets, clippers, and miscellaneous equipment.

Longeing Equipment

If your child's instructor teaches longeing—an important part of every well-rounded horseman's education—then you will also be purchasing longeing equipment. You'll need a longe whip, a longeline that is at least thirty feet long, and a longeing cavesson featuring hinged metal plates with rings attached, positioned over padding on the noseband. The cavesson can be made from good leather, in which case it will be extremely expensive, or from nylon, in which case it will be entirely affordable. The correctness of the design is what matters, and your child's instructor will be able to guide you in your selection.

Later still, if you lease a horse with an option to purchase it, or if you look for and purchase a horse for your child, you'll make a bigger investment in equipment for your child and for that particular horse.

Bridle and Saddle

The most important item will be a saddle that fits the horse and your child. If it doesn't fit, they will both be uncomfortable. There's an art to fitting saddles to horses, and your child will need some professional help with that, but you can help select a saddle that fits the child herself. If it's too small, she won't have enough room to be comfortable, and she'll tend to pop up out of it. If it's too large, she will float around in it. If it isn't balanced correctly, she will never be able to achieve a good position with her heels directly

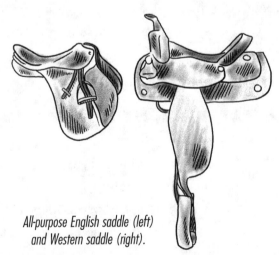

All-purpose English saddle (left) and Western saddle (right).

under her hips. This is a disaster because she'll always be sitting, chair-fashion, "behind her leg," fighting a constant battle to retrieve her balance and get her legs underneath her body.

Saddle size will vary according to the type and style of both the saddle and the physique of the rider. Your 5'5", 140-pound sixteen-year-old daughter might need an 18" dressage saddle and a 17.5" jumping saddle. For Western riding, she would need something closer to a 15.5" saddle, and if she chose to ride saddle seat, she might need a 20" seat.

Young girls and especially teenagers can be very size conscious and worry more about numbers than about actual fit; this is a bad idea where clothing is involved, and an even worse idea where saddles are involved. If your child is overly concerned with numbers, you may need to remind her that the number size of a saddle has very little to do with the size of the rider's rear end but a great deal to do with the length of the rider's thigh bones.

The saddle, new or used, will require fittings:

1. A girth with elastic at one end (this is meant for the horse's comfort, but also makes it easier for youngsters to fasten a girth).
2. Stirrup leathers (well made from good leather—they are an investment in safety and cheap ones are dangerous)—stirrups with rubber pads (wide enough to leave one-quarter of an inch clearance on *both* sides of the rider's boot).
3. Two saddle pads (one to wash and one to use on alternate days).

She will also need:

1. A bridle of a suitable size and type for the horse.
2. Reins that fit her hands comfortably (neither too wide for her to

close her hands comfortably nor so narrow that she has to make hard fists to hold them).

3. A good-quality, simple snaffle bit that fits the horse's mouth in all dimensions.

Snaffle bridle for English riding; low-port curb on Western bridle for Western riding.

When the time comes for you to buy a saddle and bridle, you should be able to enlist the aid and advice of your child's riding instructor. She's bound to know what's available in the area (used tack can be a great investment) and can warn you about poor-quality brands of new tack.

Q & A

Q: My daughter needs a saddle for her horse, and another girl at her barn is selling one that their instructor thinks would be a good saddle for us. I've seen the saddle, and it's not very pretty, the leather is worn, the color on the flaps is dark where the stirrup leathers have rubbed it, and there are scratches on the flaps and the seat. I'd like to get something that looks a little nicer, and I've seen some very pretty saddles at the tack shop that don't cost much but are brand new. In fact, they cost less than half the price of this used saddle. The new ones are $250 and this used one is priced at $550. Wouldn't it make more *sense for us to buy a brand-new saddle that looks good? I wonder if the instructor is going to get a commission on the sale, and that's why she would want us to buy the old saddle.*

A: How much commission could there possibly be on a $550 saddle? Don't forget: this instructor teaches your daughter too and will have to deal with the consequences if she recommends a saddle that isn't right. Used saddles do tend to look like the one you've described, but "used" doesn't mean "abused," and if the instructor, who knows about horses, saddles, and children, says that this saddle will be suitable for your child and your child's horse, I think you should listen.

The saddles that you saw at the shop are probably made in India and aren't worth anything at all. Their construction and materials are inferior, and they won't allow the horse to move comfortably or the rider to ride comfortably. Brand new is not always good, and if you have a choice between a cheap, shoddy, brand-new saddle and an expensive, well-made, used saddle, your choice should be clear.

Good saddles hold their value. The saddle your daughter wants may seem expensive at $550, but if it's a good-quality saddle in good shape, the price is perfectly reasonable and could be higher. With some makes of saddles, the quality has gone down over the years and an older saddle is worth more than a new one. With others, the quality has stayed good and the prices have gone up.

Have you checked to see what the new model of this saddle would cost today? Don't be surprised if the price is in four figures; you may be able to buy a used Courbette or Stuebben for $550, but the same model bought new today might cost you $1,500 to $2,000 or more.

One more thing: If your daughter ever wants to sell her good, used saddle, you shouldn't have any trouble getting your $550 investment back. The cheap Indian saddle, on the other hand, might bring you $50 or so.

The bottom line, though, isn't money, it's safety. You want your daughter riding in a saddle that's not going to cause an accident by hurting the horse or falling apart at a dangerous moment. For safety's sake, stay away from the Indian-made saddles and go for the quality item made in Germany, Switzerland, or England.

Q: My daughter came home last night and said that her young horse has outgrown his saddle and needs one with a bigger tree. I've heard this expression many times but still have no idea what it means. I'm assuming that it refers to the measurement between one side of the saddle and the other, but why on earth is it called a tree?

A: Saddles are constructed on a basic frame called a "tree," the function of which is to keep the saddle (and the rider's weight) from pressing directly on the horse's spine, which cannot bear the pressure, and instead to put the pressure on the long muscles on each side of the spine, which can bear pressure. The tree can be made from wood, metal, plastic, or a combination of those materials.

On a horse with a wide, flat back, a narrow tree would impinge on his spine and pinch him just behind the shoulders, whereas a wide tree would allow more room and allow the bearing surface of the tree to press on muscle rather than bone. On a horse with a narrow back and prominent withers and spine, a wide tree would allow the saddle to press directly on the withers and spine, causing great pain and eventual injury to the horse's back. A narrow tree would keep the pressure off the withers and spine and allow the horse to move comfortably.

Q: My son went to a horse and tack auction with his best friend and his parents. He came back with a set of stirrup leathers and a pair of stirrups that he had bid on and purchased for $7! Now he wants to use "his" leathers on the saddle when he takes his lessons. His instructor said, "No way." I think it's important for children to develop independence and self-confidence. Going to this auction and bidding was an important step for my little boy. How can I get his instructor to understand a little more about child psychology so that she won't undermine his self-esteem?

A: You do need to talk to the instructor, but not about your son's self-esteem. Children love auctions and bidding and actually getting something at the auction was probably enough reward and fun in itself. Even adults frequently bid more than they should or bid for items they don't actually need or even really want, just because they get caught up in the competitive aspect of it all. Auctions are fun, bidding is fun, and when you pay a little money for something at an auction, you'll often come home and find that you got full value for your money.

Your son now owns a pair of stirrup leathers made in India, and a pair of stirrups that are probably made from nickel. Use the stirrups as paperweights, and perhaps you'll find a use for the leathers, but don't take them back to the barn.

Stirrup leathers connect the stirrups to the saddle. Stirrup leathers need to be well-made, from good-quality, well-tanned leather, so that they are strong and a little bit stretchy. Stirrup leathers made from inferior, poorly tanned leather, and badly stitched with inferior thread are very dangerous items to attach to a saddle, because rather than giving a bit under pressure, they tend to snap. Imagine this happening at a canter or over a jump.

You wouldn't let your riding instructor come to your house and exchange your car's seatbelts for some nifty $7 ones she picked up at an auction, would you? She's not rejecting your son or you, she's simply doing her best to keep her student safe by refusing to use inferior, dangerous tack. That's part of her job.

CHAPTER 6

Good Instruction: Your Number One Priority

You cannot overestimate the influence, effect, and overall importance of your child's riding instructor. This riding instructor will be your ally in your child's education. There are many answers to the question, "What will my child get from riding lessons?," and all of them depend primarily upon the instructor.

THE ALL-IMPORTANT INSTRUCTOR

Talk to riders who got off to a bad start. "Looking back, I have to say that my first three years of riding lessons were just a waste of money for my parents. Nobody groomed the horses unless we did it ourselves, the instructors never knew who we were or paid any attention to us. We were so horse crazy that we never noticed that our parents were paying so that twelve of us kids could sit on these overworked, skinny horses and just go around and around a ring for an hour, pretty much totally unsupervised. I don't ever remember a 'lesson' happening. In fact, I don't remember ever learning anything specific about horses or riding. Now that I think about it, maybe that's just as well."

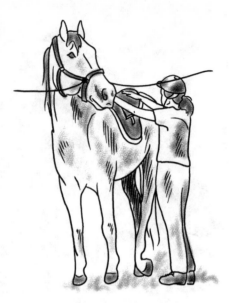

Children should learn how to handle, groom, and tack up horses.

Talk to riders who got off to a good start, and you'll hear quite a different story. "I'll always be grateful to my first riding teacher—she gave me terrific basics, and all the instructors I've ever worked with since then have told me how solid my basics are, and how good my horsemanship skills are. But really all I've done is add to and refine that first set of skills! It's been so good for me, and I feel sorry for the riders who start off wrong and have to spend years and years trying to put things right."

What Are Instructor Essentials?

Here's a checklist that will help you identify good instruction and avoid bad instruction—the personal and professional characteristics of good riding instructors. Styles and subjects may differ, but all good instructors will have

➤ a thorough knowledge of their subject

➤ a variety of ways in which to present that subject

➤ a clear awareness of their position as role models

➤ an appropriate demeanor (conduct, manners, attitude)

➤ a set of safety precautions that they always follow

➤ a set of rules that they expect their students to follow

➤ a system (logical progression) of step-by-step teaching

➤ consistency in behavior and teaching

➤ a desire to help riders learn and to help riders help themselves

➤ an unwavering focus on maintaining and creating the right skills and the right attitude in their students

FINDING A CERTIFIED INSTRUCTOR

A good instructor will be of inestimable value; an instructor who is incapable, who lacks ethics and integrity, or one who is not safety oriented, can do great harm. Protect your child by finding the best possible instructor: one with experience, credentials, and values that are compatible with those you want your child to learn.

Look for Teaching Credentials

Teaching credentials are more important than performance record. Many brilliant show riders cannot teach at all; many brilliant instructors have no show record. For your child, you need a good teacher and good communicator who understands children and horses and who will provide your child with a good foundation.

Focus on Quality

Find the best instructor you possibly can—even if you have to drive a little farther or pay a little more; it will be well worth it. In the first year or two of riding, your child is especially vulnerable and has the most need of a good teacher.

In many ways, riding is no different from any other learned skill. You would want your child to have good, correct instruction for the first year or two of anything: piano lessons, ballet lessons, baseball, reading, math.

In one way, riding is unlike any other learned skill—like dog-training, it involves learning to communicate with a member of another species. A good first teacher will not only lay the correct foundation of physical skills for your young rider, but will also instill in the students an appropriate attitude toward horses and the importance of treating them correctly and kindly. Instructors who are good with beginner riders, especially child riders, must understand children and the way their bodies and minds develop.

The safe way to lead a horse.

Go the extra mile to find the best instructor for your child—it's a decision that will have a lasting effect. And when you've selected a safety-oriented barn and a good instructor, relax and keep watching, but don't try to take over. By standing back a little, you'll show that you respect and believe in the instructor you've chosen for your child.

WHAT ARE THE BEST ORGANIZATIONS THAT CERTIFY INSTRUCTORS?

Even if you have never been interested in horses and would probably never have gone near one if your child hadn't developed this passion, you are not alone. There are groups that can provide you with much of the information you will need to help you set your standards and understand what is right, wrong, necessary, reasonable, and superfluous.

Instructor Certification Programs

There are several organizations in the United States that offer instructor certification programs and/or testing; HSA, the Camp Horsemanship Safety Association is one, and the one with which I'm most familiar is the American Riding Instructor Certification Program (ARICP). This excellent program is professionally run and exists to certify those riding instructors who are also true professionals: ethical teachers with a solid knowledge base, an absolute commitment to safety, and proven teaching skills.

Expert Evaluation The ARICP certifies instructors by evaluating them through written examinations and an oral interview. Teaching skills are evaluated by a panel that watches a videotape of the instructor in action.

Each certified instructor must recertify every five years, which involves taking the full battery of examinations again and submitting another teaching videotape for expert evaluation.

Specialty Subjects The ARICP offers certification at three different levels and in twelve specialties: combined training; distance riding, endurance, and competitive; dressage; driving; hunt seat; mounted-patrol training officer; open jumpers; recreational riding; saddle seat; sidesaddle; stock seat; vaulting.

Instructors Can Help You Find Other Instructors I strongly recommend that you contact the ARICP and ask for the list of certified instructors. If there is an ARICP-certified instructor in your area, you'll have a good starting point. If the instructors in your area have different specialties from the one you want, call them and ask them whom they would recommend.

Good instructors tend to know about one another—and they usually know who the unsafe instructors are, too. Don't expect anyone to tell you, "So-and-so is a bad, unsafe instructor," but learn to read between the lines when you ask a reliable source whether you should consider one or more of the four (for example) instructors in your area. If the answer is "Oh, they are all excellent," be happy. If the answer is "Ah, well, you might try so-and-so," with no mention of the other three, pay attention. And if the answer is "There's no local instructor I can recommend," pay very close attention indeed.

Riding Is Risky Good lessons are of inestimable value, maximizing the educational and developmental aspects of the sport while minimizing (it's not possible to eliminate) the risk. *Bad* lessons aren't worthless—they're much, much worse than that. Bad lessons are a waste of time, and they are dangerous. Riding is a risky sport; bad instruction will increase that risk by a factor of ten or more. Don't risk it.

Someday, I hope to see all good, ethical, capable riding instructors in the United States become ARICP-certified—it would provide a support system and a network of colleagues for those who achieved certification and a clear, achievable goal for those who might not achieve it on their first try. Recognized and proven competence should be just as important for riding instructors, who are in charge of the safety and welfare and education of humans and animals during riding lessons, as it is for lifeguards, who are in charge of human safety at swimming pools and beaches. That day isn't here yet, but we are working toward it.

RESOURCES

For Finding Certified Instructors

The premier riding instructor certification program in the United States maintains a current state-by-state register of certified instructors together with their specialty area, level of certification, and contact information at the ARICP Web site.

American Riding Instructor Certification Program (ARICP)
P.O. Box 282
Alton Bay, NH 03810-0282
(606) 875-4000

E-mail: aricp@aria.win.net

Web site:
http://www.win.net/aria/

CHAPTER 7

Hazards, Heads, and Helmets

D on't even consider allowing your child to ride with an instructor who doesn't require the use of safety helmets. All riders should wear helmets *whenever mounted*—at shows, in lessons, during practice rides, and when someone sits on a horse "just for a second."

SAFETY COMES FIRST

Head injuries are far too common in riding, and protective helmets can mean the difference between life and death, or between a good life and one that may not be worth living. The wearing of protective equestrian helmets will be required at any good facility: students will know that proper headgear is just part of riding.

RIDING, FALLING, AND HEAD INJURIES

If you are squeamish and can't bear the thought of your child incurring a head injury, read this anyway. It's information that you need to have. Accidents happen, and you need to know how and why head injuries occur, so you can do everything possible to ensure that your child never experiences one. Brain damage doesn't require a sharp impact on hard ground, a rock, or a tree. Even if the landing is golf-course smooth and manicured, the suddenness of the fall from a height will cause damage to an unprotected head. Children need to know that they must wear their helmets whenever they are on horseback; as a parent, you need to know more.

Children can be very persuasive when they are used to wrapping Mom and Dad around their little fingers, and they will argue like little lawyers when their wishes clash with yours. More often than not, a clash of wishes arises over the issue of safety helmets. When confronted with an angry child who wants to ride helmetless for some reason—"nobody wears them in Western, Mom!" or "I don't need it, I'm not jumping today" or "I'm only riding in the pasture bareback; it's soft out there," you'll need a strong grasp of the reality behind the helmet requirement.

What Are the Real Risks?

Intuition will tell you that jumping and galloping are more risky than quiet flatwork or trailrides or a casual meander around a pasture—and intuition will be very, very wrong. Most riding accidents occur at a walk or a standstill. The injuries you can see—lacerations and bruising from landing on something hard or sharp—are often trivial when compared to the injuries you can't see. Riders are at risk for closed-head injuries, a term that will be familiar to anyone who watches any of the popular medical dramas on television.

It's A Long Way Down The problem with falling from a height—in other words, with any head injury incurred in a fall from horseback—is not the impact of the head against the ground. Unless the rider's head lands on a sharp rock, that impact is going to be infinitely less significant than the one that causes brain damage: The impact of the rider's brain hitting the inside of the rider's skull.

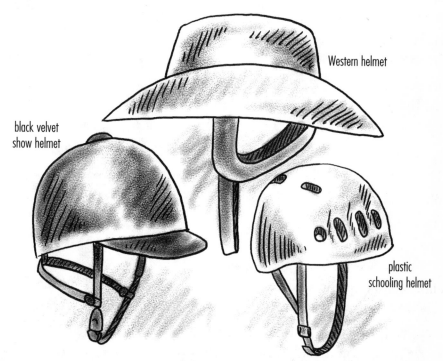

Western helmet

black velvet
show helmet

plastic
schooling helmet

The single most important part of your child's riding gear is the helmet: Use it every time, every ride.

Skulls Versus Brains When the rider's head hits the ground, the skull stops very suddenly—that's the first impact. Then the brain, still moving, slams into the inside of the skull and stops suddenly and violently. The brain is soft—the inside of the skull is hard. When the brain slams into the brain cage, two things occur, neither one of them good.

One side of the brain hits the hard surface with great force—the other side is literally torn away from the opposite side of the brain cage. The result can be badly damaged brain tissue and torn blood vessels, which leak blood. There isn't much room between the surface of the brain and the bones of the skull. If a closed-head injury (subdural hematoma) is bleeding *inside* the brain, the brain will swell and eventually press against the skull, causing damage that can endanger that person's life, as well as the quality of life that the person may have in the future.

Injuries Add Up Even an apparently mild fall, occasioning a momentary blackout or a few minutes of dizziness, can cause serious damage, and the effects of such falls are cumulative. Several head landings without a helmet can result in permanent brain damage. In more serious cases, minutes, even seconds, can literally mean the difference between life and death—or normal life and life in a vegetative state. If you have only one absolute rule about riding, let this be it. Do not allow any riding, ever, without the helmet. If your child sustains a fall and her head hits the ground, the helmet may preserve her brain and even save her life.

Helmet Importance

After any hard fall in which the helmet struck the ground, send the helmet back to the manufacturer for evaluation and for replacement if necessary. When an approved equestrian safety helmet does its job in a fall, it effectively ruins itself to save the rider's head. When the rider is wearing an ASTM/SEI approved safety helmet, the lining of the helmet compresses on impact, slowing the speed of the skull impacting against the ground so that skull and brain move at the same speed and come to a stop together. This is why the helmet *must* meet ASTM/SEI standards; this is why the helmet must be securely fastened, and this is why the helmet must be returned for evaluation after a hard fall. It's a good idea to have a second helmet on hand, so that your child can continue to ride while you wait for the results of the evaluation.

You Can't Always See the Damage The compression of the lining will not be visible to you from either the outside or the inside of the helmet, so take no chances. Most manufacturers will make replacement helmets available at a greatly reduced price—and even at full price, the cost of a new helmet is approximately that of one visit to a hospital emergency room. You'll be much happier writing that check to the tack shop.

All sports have inherent risks. The only way to eliminate the risks entirely is not to participate. But in the case of riding-related head injuries, participants can certainly go a long way to minimize the risks and the bad effects of head-first landings. We've come a very, very long way in terms of safety equipment, especially when it comes to protective helmets for riders.

How Common Are Helmets Today? The United States Pony Clubs, Inc. requires the use of ASTM/SEI certified helmets that meet or exceed the current standards for equestrian protective headgear.

Although not all 4-H clubs require helmets, more of them are requiring helmets for certain events, and the more enlightened clubs are requiring that approved helmets be worn by all riders at all times while mounted.

Approved helmets are a common sight in the huntfield nowadays, at even the biggest hunter-jumper competitions, and are gaining ground even in the dressage arena. As more riders, parents, and instructors become aware of the reasons for riders to wear helmets while on horseback, helmets will become more and more common in every equestrian sport.

Not All Helmets Are the Same Remember that horseback riding requires ASTM/SEI certified safety helmets designed specifically *for equestrians*. Bicycle helmets may be certified, but they are not suitable for equestrians. Bicycle riders who fall tend to fall forward, at speed, and on a hard surface. The injuries tend to occur to the front and top of the head, and the design of bicycle helmets reflects that.

ASTM/SEI-approved protective helmets come in different styles, and there's one to suit every riding style.

Falling from a horse is a different matter: the rider is falling from a height, and not necessarily forward. In a fall from a horse, the back and sides of the rider's head are equally at risk, and equestrian safety helmets are designed accordingly.

R E S O U R C E S

Safety Helmet Manufacturers

Lexington Safety Products
480 Fairman Road
Lexington, KY 40511
1-800-928-4287
Fax: (606) 231-8216

Lexington makes plastic schooling helmets in many colors and in velveteen or velvet-covered show-style helmets. The Lexington Lid-Locker is an outstandingly comfortable, custom-adjusting, lightweight, airy helmet, suitable for schooling in any discipline. The Lexington Woodford is a superb, low-profile velvet-covered helmet with a discreet leather-and-nylon harness, ideal for show riders.

International Riding Helmets, Ltd.
205 Industrial Loop
Staten Island, NY 10309
1-800-435-6380
Fax: (718) 356-2629

International makes safety helmets covered by Western straw hats, as well as schooling, Pro-Lite, and velveteen and velvet show helmets.

Troxel
1333 30th St.
San Diego, CA 92154
1-800-938-0155
Fax: (619) 424-4886

Troxel also makes schooling and show helmets and has recently begun offering different models to fit oval as well as round heads.

Q & A

Q: *My children ride Western, so there's not any real reason for them to wear helmets, is there? They'll look silly if they aren't wearing cowboy hats like the others, and you know how adolescents are.*

A: If the material already covered in this chapter doesn't convince you of the need for children and adults to wear helmets whenever they are mounted, perhaps this story will. It's a true one. The United States Pony Clubs National Championships and Festival is held every three years in Lexington, Kentucky. Some years ago, just before the Festival, a riding accident and head injury caused the death of a talented young dressage rider. She should have been at the National Championships with the rest of her team, having the time of her life—instead, she was dead, and her teammates were devastated. You can imagine, I am sure, the effect on her family and friends.

Pony Club requires the wearing of approved helmets, properly fastened at all times when mounted, so how did this girl incur the head injury that killed her? Did she forget to put on her helmet?

No.

She wore her helmet all the time—except when she was riding Western with her father. When the accident occurred, she wasn't going cross-country or riding in the dressage arena without her helmet, she was participating in team-penning with her father, and both of them were wearing cowboy hats. Yes, I know that helmets don't look like cowboy hats, and yes, I know how adolescents are. This particular adolescent—a talented, intelligent, beautiful girl—is dead.

If your children are going to ride, they can ride in proper headgear. Otherwise, please select another sport for them, one in which you don't mind taking proper safety precautions.

V I D E O S

Every Time . . . Every Ride . . .

This is a twenty-two minute video on head-injury prevention through the use of ASTM/SEI certified equestrian helmets. The tape is produced and distributed by the Washington State 4-H Foundation. The small investment you'll make in this tape will be a very big investment in your child's safety.

When you have the tape, ask your child's instructor if you can show it at the barn, for the benefit of all the riders and their parents. If you share it with other parents who are less well informed than you about riding risks and helmet safety, you may protect or save the lives of their children as well as those of your own.

If you'd like more information about the tape, you may contact its creator and producer, Jean Gulden, at (509) 927-9379.

The tape costs $15, postage paid, and you can pay by check, VISA, or Mastercard. The money goes to:

Washington State 4-H Foundation
7612 Pioneer Way
Puyallup, WA 98371-4570
(253) 445-4570
Fax: (253) 445-4587

Parental Involvement

You want to encourage your child to be involved, do well, enjoy, develop, and stay motivated—and this is good, but you'll need to take a different approach at different times in your child's life.

HOW CAN I BE INVOLVED WITH MY CHILD'S RIDING?

Never forget that you are in a unique position to provide something that no instructor can: the values, attitudes, and behavior at home that reinforce the best that your child learns elsewhere, including the horsemanship and sportsmanship that your child is learning at the barn. You may not be a horse expert, but you are an expert on the subject of your child, and your contribution is more valuable and will be more lasting than that of any other individual.

Providing Understanding

You can also provide something essential: understanding. As you watch your child grow and develop, you'll understand how and why your child's changing body affects balance, coordination, and stamina. It's difficult for a child to keep her balance steady on a horse when the body she's balancing isn't quite the same body she was wearing at last week's lesson. If you understand these things, you'll be able to point them out, quite casually, to your child when she is feeling clumsy and inept.

In practical terms, you are also the provider who makes your child's riding lessons possible. You provide the money for the lessons, and you provide the equipment and clothing.

Be Sensible About the Things You Spend Money On

It's easy to spend an outrageous amount of money on horse equipment and rider clothing. Spare yourself unnecessary expense by first talking to the instructor and determining what your child actually needs, what your child wants, and what your child would like you to buy if you happen to have a lot of extra money lying around the house. When in doubt about any specific item, call the instructor and ask for verification or clarification. However, if your child says, "I need my own brand-new helmet, to fit *me*, and if I fall on my head I need another brand-new helmet," the child is absolutely correct. On the other hand, if your child says, "I'm supposed to wear tall leather boots and a black coat," check with the instructor—your child may have seen this at shows or in a photograph and may even believe that this is what the instructor meant by "dress appropriately for riding," but the instructor probably had something much less costly in mind.

Double-check all equipment requests if your child is still at the lesson-taking or partial-lease stage of riding, and you hear, "I'm supposed to have a new saddle/bridle/bit for the show next month"; call the instructor and have another little chat about possible misunderstandings.

An off-hand comment about showing, even a single-syllable "Yes" answer to the question, "That saddle with all the silver and stuff, is that a show saddle?" can easily be misconstrued by a child who thought that the saddle was beautiful and is quite certain that what she heard was "You need a saddle with a lot of silver if you're going to ride in a show."

Don't call the instructor while you're still sputtering with outrage about people who blithely assume that you're made of money; chances are good that the instructor never assumed any such thing, and that she simply said, "Yes" or "Yes, it's a show saddle" or "Yes, some people have special saddles for shows" or perhaps, in answer to a completely different question, "Yes, if you want to, you may dress up for the fun show."

AT THE HORSE SHOW

The matter of horse shows is bound to arise at some point, so be ready to deal with it. Naturally your child will want to go to shows and to ride in shows, but before you say, "Oh, of course, no problem," you'll want to find out some pertinent facts.

How many shows are involved, and where are they? If you think that you are agreeing to a "fun show" or schooling show at the barn, and your child thinks you are agreeing to a full schedule of weekend shows all summer long at other venues, you're setting up a major source of conflict.

Look for the Facts

How far is the show, what are the travel arrangements, and how much money is involved? Is there a strict "no alcohol" rule on the way to the show, at the show, and on the way back from the show—and does it apply to the instructor and driver as well as to the riders? If not, you may want to limit your child's shows to those few to which you can take her yourself.

What's involved in terms of time? Is it a one-day show an hour from home? Or a two-day show two hours from home?

What sort of activities will your child be involved with, and what will your child's responsibilities be? If you send your novice-rider child to a show to learn and have fun, you don't want him to be put in charge of the other riders from his barn and expected to do the tasks that should fall to the adult instructor.

What sort of supervision is provided? Again, if *your child* is the supervisor of the others, you may want to make other arrangements.

And finally, what will your cost be?

When all these questions have been answered, you may find that you can't afford to send your child to every single show. This is not a problem, but it's something you will need to discuss. Instructors and barn managers and even your own children can make incorrect assumptions about the depth of your pockets. Talk to your child about the costs involved in showing and about how many such outings you can afford; then plan the show schedule with the instructor. Children need to understand that their parents' pockets are not bottomless, and that your own pockets may not be as deep as the pockets of some other parents.

If the instructor and barn staff take all the responsibility at the show, as they should, or if parents are not allowed to help out (for example, at a Pony Club Rally), take advantage of the opportunity to sit, watch, and enjoy. You'll have more fun if you're prepared.

NEW AND USED CLOTHING

Children outgrow clothing long before they wear it out; the bills can be very high if you purchase the best of everything and purchase everything new. With the single exception of safety helmets, which *must* be purchased new, everything else can be safely purchased used. You can't assume that a used helmet is intact, or that it meets the *current* standards, so don't take chances.

HORSE SENSE

Having Fun as a Spectator

Here are some items that will make your experience more enjoyable:

For hot weather shows have the following:

- seat cushions for bleachers
- your own chairs
- sunscreen
- sunglasses
- a sun hat
- a cooler with cold drinks

For cold-weather shows:

- heated cushions for bleachers
- your own chairs (and heated cushions)
- a blanket to put over your legs
- gloves
- a warm scarf
- a warm hat
- a thermos of hot coffee, tea, or cocoa
- tissues

Spectators need their own equipment for horse shows!

B O O K S

Sew Your Own Riding Clothes by Linnea Sheppard

This is a book that can be a real boon to anyone who sews well. If your child is hard to fit, or if you aren't happy with the quality of affordable riding clothes or the affordability of quality riding clothes, this book may be the answer. You can purchase SuitAbility patterns for a wide variety of Western and English schooling and showing apparel.

SuitAbility Web site: http://www.SuitAbility.com/ E-mail: Linea@stormnet.com 1-800-207-0256

Look for sales at tack stores; look for used clothing and equipment in the classified ads in your local paper. Read the notices posted on the bulletin boards at local barns, feedstores, and tack stores. Put up your own "Item Wanted" ads. Visit thrift stores and keep your eyes open at swap meets and garage sales. There are wonderful bargains to be had, and you're going to need them.

WHAT ABOUT PHYSICAL HELP?

You can certainly provide physical help when it's needed. The small and young will need physical help cleaning hooves, bridling tall horses, and adjusting the saddle properly. Stand back and let them do as much as they can manage alone, but if they can't quite do something, step in before they become frustrated and angry.

Do this for the sake of your child and for the sake of the horse. When children are frustrated by such a task, the horses usually bear the brunt of their anger. Accidents are more likely when children are pushed past their limits: A child who isn't tall enough to lift the saddle off the horse will pull it across the horse's back and may hurt the horse's spine; a child who can't quite manage to put a saddle back onto a tall rack may drop the saddle and cause damage to valuable equipment.

Learn How to Help

If you want to help out in the best possible way, ask your child's instructor to give you a lesson—not a riding one, but a ground-handling, grooming, tacking-up, where-things-should-be-put lesson. Even if you already know how to do these things, you'll find out how the instructor wants them done and how your child is being taught to do them. And you'll be able to understand exactly what to do when your child does ask you for help.

Helping Your Older Child Older children will need less help from you and should be able to prepare for and clean up after their horse activities alone or with help from a peer. But they may need help on special occasions—a clinic or a show—and you'll be better able to

Parents are sometimes asked to hold a horse for a moment—but if you're not dressed for it, say "no."

73

offer meaningful help if you have your own checklist and can assure yourself that the child has packed everything necessary for the day or weekend.

Q & A

Q: *We've recently moved to a different state. My kids have always loved horses, and now that we live half a mile from a boarding stable, they are both taking lessons, and they are both in Pony Club. I've never had anything to do with horses, but I signed up to take treats for the next Pony Club mounted meeting, and I want to show my support by taking a treat for the horses, too. What would be good?*

A That's a great idea. A bag of apples would involve the least work on your part, but if you want to do something extra special, put carrot sticks or other treats into individual plastic bags. The children will love the idea, the horses will love the treats, and you'll be very popular.

Q: *I feel as though I'm always at work, going to work, or coming back from work, with no time at all for myself and very little for my kids. They're good boys, and they seem to understand this, but I feel bad when all I can do is drop them at the barn for their lessons and pick them up again afterward. I'm working on an extra project to pay for the lessons, and I don't resent it, in fact I'm happy to do it, because I love my boys and they love their lessons. But I feel left out when they say "Martha (their instructor) says this" and "Martha says that." Sometimes I think they are closer to their riding teacher than they are to me. I know I shouldn't resent this, and I like and respect*

H O R S E   S E N S E

Basic Rules of Horse Handling

Never sneak up on a horse—speak to him before you touch him, touch him before you move past or around him. Horses are prey animals, and their instinct tells them to act defensively when surprised (even if they've known a person for years) by running, lungeing, or kicking. When you speak, speak softly, and when you move, move quietly and smoothly. When you touch, don't slap or tickle—use a calm, firm, reassuring stroke. Begin with the neck just in front of the left shoulder (most horses are accustomed to being handled from the left). Also don't stand directly in front of a horse: You are in his blind spot, and he cannot see you. Don't stand directly behind a horse: You're in his other blind spot, and he may step back on you or kick if startled.

If you stand close to a horse, remember that he cannot see his own feet and that it is your responsibility to keep your feet out from under his. For the same reason, never enter a barn or field, or go near a horse, wearing sandals or in bare feet. Pumps aren't much better. Good leather boots or strong, reinforced riding sneakers are best.

If you are holding a horse, stand at his left shoulder and keep a double grip on the leadrope, your right hand holding it about eight inches below his chin and your left hand holding the rest of the folded (*never* coiled, looped, or wrapped) leadrope in front of your body.

If you are leading a horse, stay at his left shoulder with the leadrope held as above and time your walk so that your right leg moves forward with his left front leg. This will help you avoid being stepped on.

If your child hands you a tacked-up horse to hold while she goes to get something, be sure that the reins are over the horse's head so that you can hold them just as you did the leadrope. Also be sure that the stirrups are run up the leathers, not hanging down; if the horse were to move suddenly, the stirrup could strike and injure him. (This is true any time the rider is not in the saddle with feet in the stirrups.)

If you feed the horse a treat—a piece of sugar, a peppermint, a slice of apple or carrot—always offer the treat on your palm, hand extended in front of you with palm flat and fingers together so that the horse—who can't see a hand under his muzzle—will not mistake your finger for a snack.

Martha and her skills and values; she's a good woman, but it bothers me. She seems to be more important in their lives than I am.

A: It's not easy to balance work, children, and the activities they always seem to have after school. It's not easy to take on extra work to pay for extra activities for the children. You've managed all of that, so congratulations—you're obviously a hard worker and a good mother.

Try to put the situation in perspective. No one can take your place as your sons' mother. Your children know that you work hard to provide them with those riding lessons, and they will appreciate this more and more as they get older and understand more about life. If they get into the car and immediately start babbling about "Martha," they're not implying that she is taking over your role; they are just sharing their joy and excitement with you and telling you what they've learned that day.

Riding instructors occupy a central position in the lives of their child students, for a lot of reasons. First, they have horses and know how to ride and are therefore to be admired. Second, they are teaching the children something that the children actually want to learn. Third, they are teaching one-on-one, dealing directly with each child, and providing personal, individual attention.

Who, besides yourself, is able to provide your children with regular individual attention? Grandparents, of course, but they aren't always around on a daily or weekly basis. Teachers in school—probably not, since class size makes it very difficult for most teachers to provide individual attention.

There's another factor here, too: Riding teachers teach children to be in control of something and not just a toaster or even a computer, but something large and alive. This isn't something that most children experience very often, and it means a lot.

You're lucky to have a "Martha" in your world. No child can ever have too many caring, concerned adults in his life. Martha is your friend and ally, not your competition. She's giving your children attention that they need and lessons that they want, but this is all happening only because of you—*you* have made it possible. Your children won't forget that, and you shouldn't either.

CHAPTER 9
A Horse of Her Own—To Buy or Not To Buy

This moment is bound to arrive—you'll feel it coming from the very first moment your child figures out that horses are the be-all and end-all of her existence. Don't be in a hurry to say "yes," and don't feel guilty for saying "later"—or "no." Owning a horse is a responsibility that a child needs to work up to gradually; owning a horse is a privilege that a child needs to earn.

MY CHILD SAYS SHE'S READY FOR A HORSE OF HER OWN. IS SHE?

It's also simply not possible for every horse-crazy child to own a horse, and in many cases it's not necessary. Parental guilt can drive you to make the wrong decision. If you find yourself feeling guilty because you have to drive for an hour or more to take your child to her weekly lesson, because she isn't ever allowed to spend the entire day "hanging out" at the barn, and because it's difficult to take the time to drive her to her monthly Pony Club mounted meeting, step back, and put the situation in perspective.

You are not a bad parent or a bad provider because you aren't able to give your child a horse of her own and a chance to ride every day; you are a wonderful parent and a good provider because you have managed to make it possible for your child to have horses in her life and to learn to ride.

Step One: Lessons

Even if you can easily afford a horse and its upkeep, don't buy one yet. Your child needs to take riding lessons for a year or so first. She will develop her skills, test her interest and commitment, and, if she is truly interested, she will use the time to learn as much as she can about riding and horses. Meanwhile, you will use the time to watch her development, evaluate the value of horses in her life, and determine the practicality of possible horse ownership.

Overloaded with Activities Some children become proficient riders and enjoy horses very much, but simply have too many other interests and too many demands on their time to make horse ownership practical. An accelerated school program, sports, clubs, music lessons, and other after-school activities can all create a situation in which a child doesn't have enough hours in the day to make horse ownership realistic. In such cases, having full responsibility for a horse will only place more demands on the child than the child can handle, and the result will be frustration, unhappiness, and eventually the retirement or sale of the horse.

"Mom's Horse" In other cases, the responsibility for caring for the horse devolves on the young rider's parents, either continually or intermittently. Just as the puppy often becomes "Mom's dog" when school interferes with daily walks and the feeding schedule, the horse can become "Mom's horse" if it lives at home, or a more expensive horse on a barn-provided care schedule if it lives elsewhere. Keep all of these thoughts in mind, and don't be in a hurry to take on this responsibility.

Step Two: Part-Leasing a Horse

If a year or more of regular lessons create a proficient young rider who is still utterly addicted to horses, the next logical step is not a purchase but a part-lease. With the approval of your child's trusted instructor, you can look for a horse (probably one purchased by parents whose child is now very busy in school) that is available on a part-time basis.

What Is "Part-Leasing"? A part-lease on a horse means that your child will, for a fee (often half of the horse's monthly board and half of its shoeing and routine medical expenses), have access to a horse to ride two or three days each week. This provides a useful preview to the idea of horse ownership. In lessons, the horse may have been brought out saddled and bridled and ready to ride; your child's part-leased horse will need to be groomed and tacked up by the child herself, and untacked, brushed, and returned to the stall or pasture after the postride cooldown.

It May Be Enough . . . or Not For many children, this much riding may be enough; it provides an opportunity to get to know a particular horse and to enjoy grooming and riding it and looking after it several times each week. If it is enough for your child, congratulations:

It's generally not difficult to find a suitable horse to part-lease. If it's not enough, and after several months of part-leasing a horse your child still wants to ride daily, it will be time for you to take the next step: a full lease.

Step Three: Full-Leasing a Horse

Again with the help of your trusted instructor, you should be able to find a suitable horse for a full lease. Under the terms of most full leases, the horse will be completely in your care. You will agree to provide farrier and vet care (usually specified by the owner) and to keep the horse on a regular deworming program (usually specified by the owner).

Know the Terms of the Lease Your child's activities with the horse will be limited by the requirements of the horse's owner: Some leases specify at what stable the horse may be kept and under what conditions (stall, twenty-four/seven field turnout, stall and paddock, etc.). Some leased horses may leave the premises for a show or clinic; some may not. Discuss the lease terms thoroughly, so that the horse you lease and the conditions of the lease are best suited to your child's actual needs.

Know Whether Horse Ownership Is for You By the time you have full-leased a horse for six months or a year, you'll have a clear idea of what sort of time and expense is involved in horse ownership. If the time requirement doesn't faze you and the expense isn't too onerous, and if your child is able to handle the requirements of schoolwork and extracurricular activities as well as meeting the obligations to the horse, it will be time to consider purchasing a horse of your own.

Q & A

Q: *My daughter Alison is thirteen. She started taking lessons three years ago, then last year we leased a horse for her. She likes the horse, but she never seems to do anything with it or even take it out of its stall. It isn't neglected, I pay the board and that includes stall cleaning and daily turnout, but I don't believe she's getting anything out of the lease.*

Alison is pushing me and her dad to buy her a horse of her own. I'm not so sure that this is the right time. Alison still goes to her weekly lessons, but she doesn't do any riding in between, and she only goes to the barn on lesson days, so the lease is a waste of money. If she wanted to renew it when it runs out I would probably say, "No."

She says that she'll start going to the barn every day and riding a lot if she has her own horse, and that it's just not fun when the horse doesn't belong to her. I'm worried that if I buy her a horse, I'll be supporting it forever while it lives in a stall at the boarding barn and Alison sees it once a week. Do you think that owning a horse could make such a difference?

A: I think it's very unlikely. Kids who love horses and riding and who are strongly motivated to ride and to spend time around horses don't have to be pushed to go to the barn, they have to be dragged away from it, kicking and screaming, when it's time for supper. They'll love a horse because it's a horse, not because it's a horse that belongs to them, and they'll take every opportunity to ride, bathe a horse, clean tack, or do anything that lets them spend more time around the horses.

Alison obviously isn't strongly motivated to ride or to be around horses—perhaps she just likes the idea of horses, or the *idea* of horse ownership, or both. But that's not a reason to purchase a horse.

Have a long talk with Alison's riding instructor and see whether you can find out what has changed since that first year of lessons. You may find that nothing has changed and that Alison likes her lessons but doesn't feel any great urge to ride between lessons. It's quite possible that you could let the lease expire and buy a horse or let the lease expire and then not buy a horse, without changing Alison's riding schedule at all. It's possible that she would be happier with twice as many lessons and no horse to look after.

Not every child likes riding; not every child who likes riding is going to want a horse; not every child who wants a horse should have a horse. Don't buy a horse for someone who doesn't ride or look after the horse she's leasing. It would be a waste of your money, and it won't be good for Alison or for the horse.

If you make a statement to your daughter along the lines of "I won't buy you a horse unless you're riding the leased one every day," expect a brief flurry of activity for a week or perhaps two weeks. But don't race out to purchase a horse based on a week or two of drastically different behavior on her part. See what the situation is in a month or two.

It's important to know your child. Some latch onto an idea or project and never let it go, and others become briefly fascinated by something and then lose interest and move on to something else. Childhood is a time to try new activities and find out which ones provide temporary fun and which ones provide lasting enjoyment, but the difference doesn't lie so much in the activities themselves as it does in the energy and commitment that the child brings to them.

Look in the basement and in the backs of your daughter's closets (with her permission, of course). If you find unmade models, assembled but unpainted models, a catcher's mitt and a soccer ball and a pair of ice skates and a trampoline and a swimsuit and a leotard, look at them and consider how desperately she wanted to

*Know your child: If she already has a room full of unused sports epuipment
and clothing, will she be any more serious about a horse?*

participate in those activities and how quickly her interest died. If
you have a piano in the living room that hasn't been tuned in
three years and is serving as an auxiliary magazine rack, think
about that, too. You don't have to follow up on every interest
expressed by your child, and when you do choose to help her pursue a particular interest, you shouldn't begin with a maximum
committment. Lessons, yes—leasing, yes, and you've tried that,
and it wasn't successful. Owning a horse—no.

*Q: Mandy, my daughter, is twelve. She's been taking riding lessons for
three years and shows no sign of outgrowing the interest. If anything,
she's becoming more interested—if that's possible! But she just doesn't
seem to have any interest at all in going to shows. She spends hours
every day riding and grooming the horses at her instructor's barn,
and I've found her sitting in their stalls or in the field talking to the
horses on more than one occasion.*

When she was in grade school, she had an imaginary friend, which I guess a lot of kids do, but Mandy's friend was an imaginary horse. I started her in lessons because I thought a real horse would be better than a pretend one, and I also thought that she might grow out of the horse obsession if she spent enough time with real ones.

Well, obviously I was wrong about that. But what puzzles me is that she doesn't want to show. Her instructor says, "Some kids don't," but does that seem normal for a rider, since she spends all her time with horses? She'll move heavy hay bales that I wouldn't even try to lift, and she'll scrub water buckets and clean out the stalls, and help the vet when he sews up wounds and floats teeth and does all sorts of other messy things, but she doesn't want to get dressed up and go to a show. Wouldn't it be more normal if it were the other way around?

A: Mandy sounds quite normal to me and also sounds like an excellent candidate for horse ownership. Showing doesn't matter unless the rider wants to do it and enjoys doing it. Horse care matters—horses need attention, exercise, clean bedding, water, food, and vet care when it is required.

Riders ride. Horsemen care for horses. Some horsemen are also riders, some riders are also horsemen, but you don't necessarily get both in one package. Mandy may be a rider—I don't know—but she's obviously a young horsewoman, which is much more meaningful. She's already doing everything, so why not let her have the pleasure of owning a horse? Showing isn't an issue or a concern, and she's shown that she's not afraid to take on the responsibility or the routine that horse ownership requires.

CHAPTER 10
The Cost of Horse Keeping

The time to estimate and plan for the expenses of horse keeping is before, not after, you purchase a horse. While you are still leasing a horse for your child, track the total costs associated with that horse. This will give you a good idea of the monthly amount associated with horse ownership. Apart from the initial purchase of the horse and basic tack, horse-keeping costs tend to fall into reasonably predictable expense categories.

HORSE-KEEPING COSTS

Monthly
- board
- extra hay and grain
- supplements
- stall cleaning
- turnout
- grooming

Monthly to Bimonthly
- farrier

Every Two Months
- deworming paste

Every Six Months
- routine veterinary exams
- vaccinations
- tooth floating (if needed)
- sheath cleaning (for geldings)

Don't Forget About the Extras

This doesn't take into account any equipment or clothing—or any extras such as unforeseen vet visits due to illness or injury. It also doesn't take into account the cost of lessons, schooling, clinics, transportation, show entry fees, etc. And even some of the predictable expenses can vary wildly from horse to horse—you'll be writing much smaller checks to the farrier if your child's horse is barefoot than if it requires special therapeutic shoeing. Similarly, a horse that's an "easy keeper" may do very well on the barn ration and never require extra feed, whereas a "hard keeper" may need extra feed every day, year round. Supplements and medications are another category in which prices can vary.

Estimating Expenses

Expenses can vary widely in different parts of the country, but it should still be possible for you to collect information about typical monthly costs in your area. A simple survey of area barns should get you the information you want:

$150–$600   monthly board payment
$30–$200   farrier
$10–$15   deworming paste
$10–$20   vet fall and spring visits ($120–$240 cost amortized over twelve months)
$100–$200   lessons (once a week at $25–$50/lesson)
TOTAL: $300–$1035 per month

What Are Basic Expenses? Basic board cost does *not* necessarily include anything beyond the stall itself and a set amount of feed. Barns vary, but some charge extra for any feed beyond what is considered "basic" at that establishment. You can expect to pay more ($20–$50) each month for a paddock or for turnout. You may be charged extra ($40–$50 or more) for someone to clean the stall.

What Are Extra Expenses? You can expect to pay more for any extra lessons or schooling sessions, any vet care beyond the twice-yearly routine visits, or any tack or equipment. Other expenses to consider:

clinics, riding clothes, trailering costs, show entries, stabling fees, and registry and association dues.

If your child decides to clean her own stall (some barns don't allow you this option) and exercise her own horse daily, you must keep in mind that you will need to arrange to pay someone else to do these things when she isn't able to.

EQUIPMENT COSTS

A good used saddle, if you can find one, will cost anywhere from $400 to $800; new, it will cost at least $1,000. It isn't unusual to pay $1,500 for a well-made, good, durable new saddle by a reputable manufacturer; $2,000 is not a shocking number. A good-quality bridle will cost you $100–$200. A bit will be another $30–$50. Basic grooming and stable equipment (halter, leadrope, curry, brushes, hoofpick, etc.) adds up: Plan on another $100 or so to complete your "starter set."

It all adds up.

The initial purchase price of the horse is basically irrelevant. The old saying, "It costs as much to keep a bad horse as it does a good one," is not quite true—a bad horse will generally cost more, simply because you will be spending more each month on feed, vet care, shoeing, schooling, and so on. A horse that is lame—no matter whose fault it is—will take a lot of care and time with no riding involved; are you ready to go to the barn two or three times a day for a couple of hours if your horse needs cold- or hot-packs and handwalking? Are you prepared to do this for a month, two months, or longer? (Consider that you may have a vacation planned, for example.) If you can't possibly do this yourself, is there someone absolutely reliable who will do this for you? Are you prepared to pay for their time?

If none of these matters are obstacles, congratulations, you're ready to buy that horse! Your child will be delighted.

HORSE SENSE

The People on Your Payroll

The cost of the horse may seem large, but it's a one-time expense. Plan ahead for the regular costs of horse maintenance. As long as you lease or own a horse, you'll be writing checks to quite a few people, so be prepared to have regular financial dealings with

- barn manager (board)
- farrier (shoeing)
- veterinarian (routine and emergency medical care)
- instructor (lessons)
- organizations (membership dues)
- shows (entry fees, stall rental, hotel)
- tack shops and catalogues (tack and clothing)
- horse supply catalogues (deworming paste, supplements, shampoo)

This isn't to say that you shouldn't buy a horse, just that you should think very hard about everything that's involved before you do it. It's a lot like having a baby to look after—it needs at least a couple of hours of care every single day of every single week, no matter how you are feeling or what you happen to be doing at the time.

HORSE SENSE

A Three-Step Approach to Horse Ownership

If you are unsure, but still want to try, start by getting your feet wet, so to speak. Begin your journey toward horse ownership and horsekeeping by leasing or part-leasing a horse first. This can teach you a lot about yourself and the amount of money/time/effort you will actually put in—without the responsibilities of actual ownership. Many people who own a horse find that they don't have enough time for it and that they would like to share the expenses with someone else in exchange for riding privileges. This means, depending on the owner, the barn, and the terms of your particular arrangement (always put it in writing) that you might be riding twice a week in exchange for grooming and stall cleaning those days, or you might have the full care of a horse whose owner is not around. There are all kinds of leasing arrangements.

HER HORSE MAY BECOME YOUR HORSE

How old is your child? If she is a young teen, owning or leasing a horse means that you or someone else will need to drive the child to the barn and wait for her there or return for her later. An older teen may be able to drive herself, which probably means finding her a vehicle of her own.

An older teen will also probably be going to college in a few years, at which point her horse will become your horse for the duration unless you, your child, your child's instructor, and another set of parents and their child can work out a suitable leasing arrangement. Not all leases are satisfactory; not all leases last. Your college-bound daughter may plan to retrieve her horse in four years, but in the meantime, it may very well end up as your horse. It's important that you factor in that possible expense, and it's important that you like the horse too.

Q & A

Q: Before I even think about buying my child a horse, I want to be absolutely sure that I can afford to maintain it no matter what. When I was twelve I had a horse for one year, then we had to sell it because it cost more than my parents thought it would. I was miserable about it for years, and I won't put my child through that. How can I be sure that this won't happen?

A You can't predict the future—accidents, emergencies and illnesses, job changes, and many other factors can affect your ability to keep a horse. Assuming that life remains relatively uneventful, though, it's certainly possible to make a fairly accurate estimate of how horse-keeping expenses will affect your finances.

The easiest way to do this is simply to visit the local barns, and when you've found one or more that you like, ask about their rates. Find out what's included and what's extra. Then find out what the other horse-associated expenses will be—as discussed earlier in this chapter. When you have a total, round off the sum (up, not down), open a separate savings account, and start to put that amount into the account every month.

After six months or, preferably, a year, ask yourself whether it has been easy or stressful to do without that money. If the answer is "stressful," then you're not ready to afford the expenses of horse keeping. If the answer is "easy," then you are, and you already have a financial cushion for those occasions that require extra money immediately—something that's inevitable wherever a horse is concerned.

Q: My family has two horses that are boarded at a barn about twelve miles away. It has some turnout areas but they aren't very big. We're not happy with this arrangement, because we believe that horses should be kept in as natural a state as possible. We would like our horses kept outdoors in a pasture, and we're about to make that happen.

A month ago, we bought a house outside of town. It has four fenced acres that used to be cattle pasturage. The fencing is barbed wire, and I know that's bad, but the field is a really big one and the horses would have no reason to go near the wire. We plan to replace it, a piece at a time, with new fencing that's more suitable for horses, maybe plain high-tensile wire (no barbs). My question is, how safe would it be to bring the horses home soon and use the money that we're spending on board to put up the new fencing? If we have to take out the barbed wire and then put up another fence, it'll be a long time before we can bring the horses home. If we take a chance on the barbed wire (which we will be steadily replacing), we'll be able to have the horses at home where we can keep an eye on them.

A: You're going to have to be patient. Get rid of all that barbed wire before you bring any horse onto your property. Even if this means boarding your horses for an extra six months, it will cost less than the vet bills that come from mixing horses and barbed wire. If you have all your fencing replaced except for one twenty-foot section back behind the trees at the far end of the pasture, any horses turned out in the pasture are guaranteed to find that wire and hurt themselves.

Don't use high-tensile wire either, unless you get the kind that's embedded in highly visible, wide strips of plastic material. The second most dangerous fence for horses is high-tensile wire: Horses can't see it, and if they run between two fenceposts (and through the wire), that fence will have the same effect as a large egg-slicer.

You can budget and plan for fences in terms of materials, labor, costs, and schedule. You can't do that with vet bills, and there's a terrible, sick feeling that settles permanently in your stomach when you're paying vet bills for horses that have been injured because of something you did or neglected to do. Don't put yourselves, or your horses, through that.

Q: *All three of my children have horses now, and it's not practical for us to pay board to someone else when we have a nice barn and two pastures at home. We're going to bring them home to our place. The place hasn't had animals on it for a long time. We inherited it six months ago, and my father had sold his last horse about five years before he died.*

I've looked in all the books, and according to everything I've read, Dad did a great job with this place—the barn is perfect for four horses, and the pasture fence is V-mesh wire, about five feet tall, with big wooden posts and wooden boards across the top. I remember when he put it in, and it must have been thirty years ago at least, but it looks like new.

What I can't figure out is what he did with the manure, and what we ought to do with it. I'm afraid that he might have spread it on the fields, because he used to own several hundred acres in addition to the house, barn, and pastures. I'm guessing that it might take a year or two for us to have a problem if the horses stay in the pastures, but obviously we'll have to act sooner if they're in the stalls. Since the rest of the land isn't ours anymore and some of it is under development, I don't think we can get rid of the manure that way. What can we do? Manure means flies, and we don't want flies either.

A: With three horses and forty pounds of manure per horse per day, you won't have to wait a year to have a problem. You're going to have to contract with someone—perhaps the person who bought the several hundred acres—to haul your manure away periodically, and in the meantime, you'll need somewhere to keep it. A manure pile doesn't have to be a big, spread-out mess. It can be kept squared off and flat, and encouraged to rot and become useful to gardeners. Keeping it confined to one area, preferably an area with low walls, and keeping it covered with plastic (a black tarpaulin is ideal) will help it rot faster and create more heat, which will help kill off the fly eggs.

Talk to your county extension agent, who will be able to offer you advice and assistance and perhaps even some plans for making the best sort of manure pile for your area.

CHAPTER 11

Horse Shopping 101:
What to Look For

You've probably heard that it's better to buy a horse at some times of the year than at others. It's true: You're more likely to get a good price in the autumn. The show season is over, the horse owners are looking ahead to a winter of extra hay and frozen water buckets, and some of them are leaving for college.

WHEN AND WHY TO BUY A HORSE

Horses at boarding barns often get sold to someone else at the barn, or to someone who knows someone at the barn, but you'll find quite a few privately owned, kept-at-home horses for sale in the autumn. The price will drop to reflect the reality: Horses plus winter often equals a great deal of work for little riding.

Here's a thought to ponder: The family that's selling the horse has based their decision on the same reality that you will experience as soon as *you* own the horse. Be ready, and have a plan in place so that you won't add a great deal of work to your own day or cause a horse to suffer semiabandonment. This is where your parental responsibilities will come into the picture again.

If your child loses interest, you will need to be ready to step in and lease or sell the horse to someone who will take care of it. Horses are surprisingly delicate in many ways, and they are high-maintenance animals. Even if you have a safely fenced, perfect pasture with a run-in shed, an automatic water tank, and an enormous salt block, somebody is still going to need to check over those horses and feed them at least twice a day.

If your child has too much homework or too many after-school activities, or develops a busy social life, somebody is still going to need to feed and check on those horses twice a day. Who do you suppose that person will be? (Hint: How long did it take that puppy to become "Mom's dog"?)

FINDING THE RIGHT HORSE

Your child's riding instructor will be able to help you find a suitable horse. You might find a lovely horse on your own, but a vet check is essential—don't take a horse home without it. And since a vet check will be much more useful if the vet knows you a little and knows what you want the horse for, you will also want to enlist the help of your child's instructor.

Look for a Horse that Suits Your Child's Needs

The horse you find on your own might not suit your needs or those of your daughter, especially if she wants to show (hunters? jumpers? eventing? dressage?). The more clear you are about what you plan to do, and what you have time/energy to do, the more accurate you will be about what kind of horse you want, and the better your vet and instructor will be able to help you.

Look for an Older, Experienced Horse

A well-cared for, well-trained horse between, say, nine and fifteen years old would be a good investment. Don't buy your child a young, inexperienced animal as a first horse—everyone will be sorry. Any old-time, experienced, savvy instructor will tell you that in riding, the worst possible color combination is green-on-green. A well-trained, solid citizen horse in its teens is what you'll want for that first horse; anything that's under seven years old is unlikely to have had enough experience to be truly seasoned, and if a very young horse has had all that experience, he has been worked too hard, too early, and is less likely to remain sound.

BEFORE YOU SHOP

Before you begin serious horse shopping, do some homework. You can't learn it all, but make the effort, because everything you learn will benefit your child. Read basic horse books and basic horse-care books.

Learn as much as you can about conformation, gaits, movement, and common ailments and injuries.

There are books on every aspect of training—read a few good ones that apply to your child's particular interest (hunter shows? eventing? dressage? reining?). This will help you understand what sort of horse is wanted for each discipline and why. Read a few basic books on dressage, regardless of your child's particular interest, because basic dressage is useful for all horses and riders. It's more than techniques of riding and training—it's a methodical system of clear communication with the horse.

Things that Matter

When you purchase a horse, the price is affected by some things that do matter. The horse's age, experience, attitude, and soundness are all important factors, and you will need to find a horse that has a workable (not perfect) combination of all of these.

Age and experience matter very much indeed. Do not buy a young horse for your child, please, no matter how lovely it may be and no matter how much potential it may have. Your child is still learning, even if she has had several years of lessons and can walk, trot, canter, and jump confidently indoors and out, over all types of terrain. A young horse needs an older, experienced rider; a young rider needs an older, experienced horse.

The Clue Factor I have a personal formula for evaluating horse-rider combinations: it's called the Clue Factor. The formula is simple: horse and rider together must have enough knowledge and experience to add up to at least one Clue between them.

An older, very experienced rider has a Clue and could therefore manage a young horse with no Clue. A young, relatively inexperienced rider has a fraction of a Clue and needs a horse with a Clue: an older, well-trained, experienced animal.

A rider with several years of good lesson experience and a lot of riding hours under her belt may have half a Clue, and could, with the help of her instructor, take on a horse that has experienced only a few years of training and riding and therefore also has half a Clue.

An experienced rider could do wonderfully with an experienced horse—between them, they would have a total of two Clues. On the other hand, an inexperienced rider with an inexperienced horse would have a total of no Clues . . . you get the idea.

BOOKS

The Older Horse
by Eleanor M. Kellon

This is an essential resource for owners of horses who are over ten—it's ideal for people who are leasing a horse for their child or purchasing that all-important first horse. The book covers the purchase, care, and conditioning of the older horse, the specific problems faced by the aged equine, system by system, and the care of a retired horse. Since the first horse you purchase for your child will almost certainly be at least ten years old and possibly considerably older, this is essential reading material for you.

Things that Don't Matter

There are also things that do not matter, but that can affect price. Color is one; popular colors and flashy markings can add to the price of a horse: If white markings are fashionable and you find a horse with a blaze and four stockings, it is likely to cost much more than an almost-identical horse with no markings or a tiny star.

Suitable Size Size generally adds to the price: Buyers are often far too preoccupied with the height of a horse and refuse to consider any horse under a certain height. This is a great mistake, but it's one by which you may be able to profit. If no one in your area wants a horse that is under 16.0 hands, you may be able to find absolutely wonderful, kind, sound, well-trained horses of 15.3 and under at a very reduced price.

The Horse's Hand and Your Child's Legs The important factor in terms of horse/rider fit is not the horse's height, but the width of his barrel and how that relates to the rider's length of leg: If your child can sit comfortably on the horse in a position that will allow him to use his aids correctly, it absolutely won't matter whether the horse is 16.2 or 14.2.

Breeds and Breeding Finally, the breed of the horse may affect the price, although this shouldn't be important to you and your child unless you have ambitions to compete in breed shows. In practical terms, for everyday riding, Pony Club, and participation in open shows of any kind, it shouldn't matter in the least whether the horse is a Quarter Horse, an Arabian, a Morgan, a Thoroughbred, or a Connemara.

This is the kind of horse you want to find!
If your child's instructor likes it and the veterinarian approves, buy this one.

It may be a papered or an unpapered crossbreed; it may even be one of the disappearing group of grade horses (breeding unknown but obviously mixed), as long as it is able to remain sound and comfortable while participating in the activities that interest your child.

There are any number of suitable breeds. It can be useful to learn as much as you can about various breeds and to select from among those that are physically, temperamentally, or even historically most appropriate for your child's needs, but unless you plan to show in breed-only shows, don't focus on breed but rather on the individual.

Gender and Price Gender can also affect price: Your horse should be a gelding or a mare, not a stallion. Mares generally cost more than geldings, because they can have a second career. Horse owners sometimes prefer mares because they think that it would be nice to breed a foal from the mare if she herself becomes unable to perform as a riding horse. Since breeding and raising a foal is not at all sensible or practical for the average horse owner, and utterly impractical for anyone who boards her horse elsewhere, you will have no reason to purchase a mare. Don't reject one if you like her, but be aware that her gender may add to her price, making her more costly than an equally attractive (and probably more steady and predictable) gelding.

Geldings make wonderful first horses, second horses, third horses . . . they tend to have equable temperaments and of course no hormone-driven attitude problems. Some individuals prefer mares to geldings, but a gelding, more relaxed, more forgiving, and less sensitive than a mare, will typically make a better first horse. Stallions are impractical. They take a good deal of skill to handle in safety, require different fencing, and can't be taken to most shows. A stallion would not be suitable for a child's first horse. In fact, unless you are a breeder by profession, there is no reason for you to buy a stallion.

Necessary Compromises

When you look for a horse for a young rider, and if you insist, as you should, that the horse have a Clue, you will need to be able to make some compromises. Yes, there are some horses that have experience, talent, soundness, and not much age, but those are comparatively rare and exceedingly expensive. For most of us, some compromises will be required, and it's important to know which ones are realistic and safe.

Soundness, experience, and talent are all factors to consider. Generally speaking, more experience will mean more age, and there will be a concomitant reduction in soundness. More soundness and more talent generally mean a young horse or a terribly expensive horse that isn't quite so young.

"Manageable unsoundness" is a concept that you should discuss with your veterinarian and your instructor; it sounds horrid but it may simply mean that your child's horse cannot be raced fast or jumped high if you wish to keep him comfortable so that he can continue to give your child many years of pleasurable riding.

It may mean that the horse will remain sound with considerate riding, careful management, and regular therapeutic shoeing. It may mean that arthritis is beginning to take its toll, but that long warmups before work and regular injections of joint-

"Noble Stallion, Wild and Free"—this may be your child's dream, but it's not the horse you want for your child.

lubricant products will enable the horse to look after your child for many years to come. A horse with manageable unsoundness is not at all the same thing as a horse that is, purely and simply, unsound. When in doubt, talk to your veterinarian and ask her advice—then follow it.

Q & A

Q: We're starting to look for a horse for my daughter. She is fourteen and had a growth spurt last summer, so she is now five feet, six inches tall. I don't think she's going to get much taller than that. The horse she was riding before last summer was fifteen hands, and she was too big for him after the summer. Her feet were hanging way under his belly. Now she's convinced that she needs a horse that's at least sixteen hands, and she won't even look at anything under that height. I don't want her to buy a horse that's too small for her, but I've noticed that all of the horses that are sixteen hands and taller seem to be a lot more expensive than the shorter ones. Does she really need a horse that's at least sixteen hands, and if she doesn't, how can I get that across to her?

A: You've discovered something important: height adds to the price. Especially if a horse is wanted for hunter-jumper or dressage competition, there's a big demand for tall, very tall, and extra-tall animals. The smaller horses can and do win, but many riders are convinced that the taller the horse, the better the score. If your daughter is a competitive rider, this may be a factor in her wish for a tall horse.

Height doesn't do anything for the horse, though—smaller horses are easier to manage, are able to be comfortable in normal-sized stalls and trailers, and tend to stay sound longer. Taller horses don't jump better or perform better just because of their added height, and they carry more weight on their legs and feet that are not noticeablly larger and stronger than the legs and feet of smaller horses.

Horses and riders should fit one another, but fit is not a question of height. Your daughter needs a horse that she can sit comfortably and that has a wide enough barrel to take up her length of leg. Ask your daughter's riding instructor if she can help by letting your daughter sit on a couple of different-sized horses to see what build feels most comfortable to her.

Your daughter needs to realize that a horse can be 17 hands and have a slender and narrow build that would allow her feet to hang below its belly. Another horse could be fifteen hands and have a sturdier build and wider-sprung ribcage that would take up the entire length of your daughter's leg. If she can sit on a few horses and notice the differences, I think you'll have an easier time convincing her to look at horses between fifteen and sixteen hands.

Q: My daughter is twelve and very heavy. She's not good at most sports, although she is very coordinated and well balanced at home, so I don't know why this doesn't carry over to other activities. She won't swim any more because she doesn't want to wear a swimsuit. She is on a diet but her doctor doesn't want her to get carried away with the dieting, and even said that he would rather see her eat anything she wants and just be more active. The only sport Heather is interested in is horseback riding. We gave her a year of lessons and she did surprisingly well. She now wants a horse of her own so that she can ride every day. Is riding a good sport for a heavy person? Will it help her lose weight if she rides every day? And what kind of horse is best for a rider like Heather?

A: I'm glad that you and Heather's doctor are not pushing her to go on a strict diet. Put the focus on building her health, instead, because that's what matters. Too many girls of Heather's age are bulemic or anorexic. At twelve, Heather may be getting ready for a growth spurt and/or puberty, and in any case she is still growing. She needs to build her health and her self-esteem, and the best way to do both is to become more active.

Riding is a good sport for anyone who enjoys riding. Riding can be an especially good sport for children like Heather. Since Heather enjoys riding, continue to support her interest and efforts. There are other sports that would help her become fit more quickly, but she's far more likely to continue to participate actively in a sport that she likes, and it's the continued activity that will make the difference to her health and self-esteem in the long term. Heavy individuals can be good riders. As with any other activity, it's interest, determination, and perseverance that create success.

Work with Heather's riding instructor—she can help you find the right horse. It will be easier if you know what type of horse you are looking for: a sturdy, strong, compact horse that is well able to carry its own weight and that of a rider. Tall slender horses are not generally good weight carriers; smaller, well-built animals are much more suitable.

If you can find an old-style Morgan, similar to the ones used by the U.S. Cavalry, you'll have the ideal horse. The sort of Arabian that does well in endurance competitions would also be a possibility, and there are breeders who think that a Morab (Morgan-Arabian cross) combines the best qualities of both breeds. Another useful type of horse would be a performance-type (not halter or racing type) Quarter Horse—the kind of horse that would make a good "using" ranch horse.

Q: My son is nine, and we (my husband, Sarah, Brian's instructor, and I) agree that it's time for him to have his own horse. But we haven't been able to agree on what to get. Brian is small for his age, and we think he would do better with a pony. Sarah wants to look for a small horse, but even a small horse is a lot bigger than what my husband and I had in mind. We thought that a really small pony would be a better match for Brian physically; he could control it more easily and that would make him feel more secure. Sarah doesn't think so, and the last time we talked about it, she said that she doesn't want Brian to get a little pony because she won't be able to ride it. This doesn't make sense to me. We want to buy a pony for Brian, not for Sarah, and anyway Sarah has plenty of horses to ride. How can we resolve this? Sarah is a good instructor and Brian loves her, but we were really turned off by the idea that we should buy a horse for her to ride.

A: The only problem you have here is one of miscommunication. You heard what Sarah said, but you didn't understand why she said it or what she meant by it. Read this, and then talk to her again.

It seems logical and intuitively obvious that a very small boy would be better off riding a very small pony. I can entirely understand why you think that—but you're wrong.

A well-trained small pony is a wonderful asset to any barn and is wonderful for a small child. But—and this is a very major "but"—the key adjective here is not "small," but "well trained." A pony that is not well-trained will not be easily controlled by its rider, and if the rider is a small child learning the skills of riding, and the pony and child are in conflict, the result can be a very frightened child.

It's not enough to purchase a well-trained pony or horse; the animal's training must be kept up. Any horse or pony that is ridden exclusively by one rider will eventually rise or sink to the level of that rider. In other words, the well-trained small pony or horse will not stay well-trained if it's ridden exclusively by a small child who is learning to ride. That's why Sarah said you should get something that she could ride. If she rides Brian's pony regularly and keeps reminding it of its training, then Brian will be able to ride it, improve his riding, and rise to the pony's level instead of bringing the pony down to his level.

If you purchase a pony that is too small for Sarah to ride, its training will inevitably deteriorate until you have a badly trained small pony and a potentially dangerous situation on your hands. This won't improve your son's skills or add to his self-confidence—he truly would be better off with a larger pony or small horse.

If you feel really strongly about the size issue and want something that is in the thirteen hands region, consider purchasing a Haflinger. Although small, they can carry adults comfortably and are very popular family horses in Europe. If you're willing to consider something a little larger, consider a small Morgan. You and Sarah need to work together on this—and that means talking to one another instead of at one another. The next time Sarah says something that bothers you, smile and say "I don't understand that, can you explain it to me?" Remember, the priority for everyone should be the same: finding a horse or pony that Brian can learn on and enjoy.

CHAPTER 12

Horse Shopping 102:
Where to Look

The easiest and most obvious way to begin is by reading the ads. Start with your local paper and with whatever local-advertising paper you may also have in your area. Also look in the regional papers and in papers from large cities nearby. If your child subscribes to horse magazines, look in the classified sections.

LOOKING FOR A HORSE

If she is in Pony Club, consult the USPC News. Look for ads in the local Pony Club and riding club newsletters. Look on stable bulletin boards and on tack store and feed store bulletin boards. Ask your vet and your farrier—you should already have asked your instructor, so that she can be watching for just the right horse.

Let Your Child's Instructor Help You

When you are horse hunting, always work with your instructor. She can help you better than anyone: She knows the area, she knows the local barns, stables, horse owners, and many of the horses; she knows your child and is familiar with her individual talents and abilities and personality. She knows how your child has done in lessons and with her leased horse, and is ideally positioned to help you find the right horse.

And since she will be working with your child and the horse, she has a vested interest in getting the right one. If you have any doubts about whether your instructor has your best interest at heart, then you need to find another instructor whom you can trust and only then begin looking for a horse.

In horse ads, "prospect" means that the horse hasn't actually done whatever it is yet. Thus, a "hunter prospect" doesn't know how to jump, a "dressage prospect" may have tried and failed to learn to jump, an "event prospect" may be impossible to stop after a jump, and an "endurance prospect" may be small, thin, and unable to jump.

This is one way to look for a horse . . .

Advertising also causes horses to shrink. The 16.2 hands horse in the ad will shrink to 15.3 hands by the time you see him, the 15.2 hands horse will shrink to 14.3 hands, and so on.

"In good condition" tends to mean "extremely, dangerously overweight," whereas "very fit" can mean "seriously underweight." "Goes English and Western" usually means that the horse's owner has only a very vague idea of either style. Such horses are generally very pleasant animals that will stop, start, and turn regardless of what they are wearing or who is on board—this can be nice for casual wandering around the property, but don't be surprised if your instructor is less than impressed by the claim and by the horse.

"Great potential" is like the "prospect" horses—potential means "hasn't done it yet, but who knows, someday maybe he might." "Sensitive" and "energetic" are warnings, not praise—the horse is probably jumping out of its skin. "Calm and quiet" may mean semicomatose—it's the English equivalent of the Western term "dead broke." There are variations on that theme, too: "kid broke," "old lady broke," and "fat man broke."

"Ridden by a child" may sound ideal, since you want this horse for your child—but you'd need to see both the horse and the child who has been riding it. Horses are not necessarily improved by being ridden by children, especially unsupervised children. Take each ad with a grain or two of salt, call about the most interesting-sounding ones,

. . . but it's better to begin by talking to your child's instructor.

HORSE SENSE

Reading Horse Advertisements

Some terms don't mean what you expect them to mean, and more often than not, the horse described in the ad is unrecognizable when you meet him in the flesh. Even without lying, it's possible for people with horses for sale to write wonderfully deceptive—sorry, creative—ads.

trust your instinct if you don't like the voice or the answers at the other end of the line, and don't be in a hurry. Take all the time you need and enlist all the help you can to find the right horse for your child. When you think you've found it, look at it again, and then have your instructor try it, and then have your child try it. If it still seems like the right horse, have your veterinarian perform a prepurchase exam.

Get Information from the Horse's Owners

Talk to the horse's current owners and find out everything you can about the horse's history, habits, abilities, likes, and dislikes. If you're still enthusiastic, buy the horse. If your gut feelings tell you that you shouldn't buy this horse, don't. It will be much less traumatic to look for another horse than to try to sell the one you've realized isn't right after all, but that your child has already fallen in love with.

VISITING STABLES AND FARMS: HOW FAR TO GO

There are good reasons not to go too far when looking at horses; distance tends to add to the price, and the horse that you might be able to purchase locally for a reasonable amount may cost twice as much if you find him two states away—and then there's the shipping to consider. ...an get to them easily, you ...orses, and you can look at ...ur mind. With local horses, ...n the prepurchase exam. So ...a horse locally before you look regionally or nationally.

Look Politely

There's an etiquette to looking at horses: Look only at those that interest you, and don't ask to see the horse ridden, or to ride the horse, unless you are truly, deeply interested. If you know after five minutes that the horse is too old, too young, too green, too unsound, or the wrong shape entirely, say "Thank you for letting us visit," and go away.

Don't stay and chat endlessly—the sellers are taking time from their day to show their horse to possible buyers, and once you've decided that this horse is not for you, you're no longer in this category. People who use horse shopping as an excuse to cadge free pony rides are called "tire kickers"—not a compliment.

NARROWING YOUR SEARCH

When you've looked through the ads in the paper, checked the bulletin boards at the local barns and tack shops and the classifieds in your child's horse magazines, and gotten suggestions and leads from your instructor, begin by eliminating the obvious impossibilities. These would include horses that are too young (don't even look at that three-year-old, regardless of his appearance or "potential"); horses that have done too much at a young age and thereby endangered their soundness (the three- or four-year-old horse that is jumping three foot six inches or showing at Second Level dressage, for instance).

Cross Off the "Impossibles"

Eliminate the horses that are truly too large for your almost full-sized older child, as well as those that are too small for your lots-of-growing-left-to-do younger child. The horses that are still on your list will be the ones you should look at.

Look at the "Possibles"

When you have narrowed your search to perhaps five or six horses, arrange to look at them. If your child likes any of them particularly well, plan to go back and see those horses again. Cross the others off your list—this should narrow your search to perhaps two or three horses.

At this point, you may be ready to involve your child's instructor—who may well have recommended one or all of these horses in the first place. Pay her for her time, and ask her to try the horses that interest your child most.

How to Try a Horse

The sequence of horse trying should run as follows; first the horse's owner or regular rider should ride the horse for you while you watch. This is sometimes enough to eliminate a horse from consideration. If your child and her instructor still like the horse, have the instructor ride it and evaluate its suitability for your child. Finally, if the instructor finds the horse to be suitable, says that it can indeed do whatever it is supposed to be able to do, and that it should be able to do what your child wants it to do, then it will be time for your child to have a test ride.

What to Do If You All Like the Horse

If this goes well and you decide that you want to make an offer on a particular horse, the next step is to ask your own veterinarian or your instructor's veterinarian (never the seller's veterinarian) for a prepurchase exam. You'll want to ask your vet what's involved in the exam, what he will look for, and what the cost will be. Then, assuming that the horse passes the prepurchase exam, you can take care of the necessary paperwork, and finally make arrangements to have the horse sent back to your boarding barn.

Q&A

Q: *I want to buy a horse for my son. He is eleven and had two years of lessons where we lived before we moved. He doesn't have any friends in the new place yet, and I promised him that he could have a horse someday, so this seems like a good time to buy one. A friend who rides recommended someone she knows. I was about to call him, but another friend told me that he's a full-time horse dealer.*

Don't horse dealers have a terrible reputation, sort of like used-car salesmen? It sounds like a bad idea to me, but I don't want to offend the friend who recommended him, and I don't know any other good source of horses. If we go to look at his horses, what kind of tricks should we watch for? And wouldn't we be better off if we could buy a horse from someone who owns a boarding stable or a teaching stable?

A: If you really think that this person is unethical and dishonest and that he will try to misrepresent the horses he has for sale, don't go there at all. You won't be happy even if you find a horse you like, and if you buy the horse and it goes lame two years from now, you'll think that the dealer had something to do with it, even if he was perfectly honest and the horse was sound when you bought it.

A good horse dealer is someone whose business depends on repeat happy customers, not on one-offs or on unhappy customers who continually bring in one unsatisfactory horse to exchange for another equally unsatisfactory one. There are some corrupt and unethical horse dealers, and there are also corrupt and unethical owners of boarding or teaching stables, who will also sell you an unsatisfactory horse. You can't assume corruption or purity on anyone's part, when you have no evidence either way.

However, I think that you should deal with this in another way entirely, by putting your child back into riding lessons. He'll need to continue them anyway, whether he gets a horse of his own or not. Visiting area stables will give you and your son a chance to meet people. Finding a good local instructor who teaches children of his age will give you an ally in your search for the right horse and will give your son the chance to be around horses, to ride, and to meet other children who are the same age and share his interest in horses.

When the time is right and you're both more familiar with your new home, when you know more riders and instructors and are familiar with barns, horses, vets, and farriers in the area, when your son has local friends who ride and you have local friends whose children ride, you'll be in a much better position to start looking for a horse. At that point, you may end up visiting the same horse dealer, but perhaps you'll feel better about him if he is recommended by several people you know and respect.

Q: I'm wondering if I could find a good horse for my daughter at an auction. I've heard about some incredible bargains at auctions, and it seems to me that would be a good way to find a good horse for not too much money. And aren't most racehorses bought at auctions? We don't know that much about horses but we're learning fast, and I think I could recognize the kind of horse I'd want for my child.

A: I think that everybody has heard of those bargain horses, but hardly anyone has actually met one. Auctions can be good sources of horses if you are talking about a breeder's auction or an established auction of racehorses, but those will be high-priced, big-ticket items, and those auctions have almost nothing in common with the sort of local auction you're thinking of attending.

These local auctions tend to be the last stop before the slaughterhouse for horses that are elderly, injured, ill, or chronically lame. Although you might find a bargain—and pigs just might be circling overhead at the time—you're far more likely to find a wonderful, sweet, adorable horse that is too lame to ride and will never be comfortable again, or a calm, relaxed horse that will be a maniac when the drugs wear off and the pain returns. Don't try to find a horse for your child by visiting the local auction house. You won't find what you want, and you'll make yourself and your child very sad. Instead, ask your child's riding instructor to let you know whenever she hears of something suitable for sale.

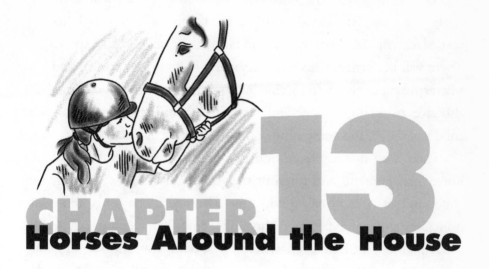

CHAPTER 13
Horses Around the House

Even if you own some acreage and are under heavy pressure to let the horse come home with your child, plan to keep the horse at a boarding barn for at least the first few years.

SHOULD WE KEEP THE HORSE AT HOME?

There is nothing like having your own horses and caring for them yourself. But don't be in a hurry. If you are new to all this, give yourselves, as a family, at least a few years before you attempt to keep your own horses.

Why Boarding Is Better at First

A good boarding barn is a much safer and more suitable environment for those first years. At a good boarding barn, there will be people to help you, teach you, lend you books and videos, and share their experiences. There will be farriers who arrive regularly to shoe the horses, and vets who arrive regularly to do routine immunizations. A good boarding barn also gives riders the chance to interact with other riders—something your child will enjoy, and something you can't provide at home.

There's an incredible amount for you to learn about horses and horse management, and for your own safety and welfare, that of your child, and of your horse, spend time where you can learn about the principles and practicalities of horse keeping. There's a good deal of participation required even when you board your horse—after all, horse care and exercise, feeding and watering are all every-single-day responsibilities—but nothing compared to what you'll need to do if you bring that horse home.

Who Will Do the Work at Home?

Will you keep the horse in a stall with an attached paddock? Fine. Some-one will need to be at that barn every day, cleaning out the stall and pad-dock, grooming the horse, turning him out, cleaning out the feed buckets and the water buckets, and then feeding and watering the horse. And that's when the horse is healthy, uninjured, and the weather is good.

Will you be able to put in the extra daily time when the horse needs daily or twice- or thrice-daily poulticing or medicating or hand walking? And what about winter? Everything takes so much longer when you have to shovel a path to the barn, push the manure wheel-barrow through the snow, and break the ice on the water buckets.

And there are the routine tasks—being there to catch and hold your horse for the farrier and treating that farrier well indeed, because farriers are always busy, and it isn't cost-effective for them to drive to someone's little barn and shoe a single horse. If you can't be there when the farrier or the vet is there, who will be? Did you plan to take a vacation—and do you have someone reliable, knowledgeable, and trustworthy who will come to stay at your home and look after your horse(s)? Will it be possible for you to pay that person *and* afford your vacation?

WE'RE BRINGING THAT HORSE HOME ANYWAY

In this case, you'll need to do more homework, and you'll need to spend more money. Don't imagine that you'll save money by keeping the horse at home—expenses have a way of balancing themselves out. If you're bringing the horse home because you and your daughter can't imagine anything more wonderful than seeing her horse from the kitchen window of your own home, then bring the horse home and enjoy it—but first, be prepared.

Read Books to Help You Prepare

Basic horse-care knowledge is quite accessible to you. Any good instructor will automatically teach this, and your daughter probably already knows it, but you might benefit from a crash course in horse management.

Consult With Your Veterinarian

Your vet will be happy to help you, too, and will know what you will need to do and buy for your horse based on where you live (climate, pasture, etc.). Your vet will also be able to suggest any changes in your property fencing—smooth, high-tensile wire works for cattle but can be quite dangerous for horses, because they can't see it unless you add some strips of plastic to make it visible.

Make Your Fencing Horse-Safe

Any barbed wire that is on your property should be long gone before any horse sets foot there. If your property is already fenced with four-by-four wire, you may be able to leave it in place, but be careful—horses have been known to stick feet through it and get badly hurt. Keep in mind that you can't safely turn shod horses out with this kind of fencing; there's simply too great a chance that they will manage to get a piece of the wire caught between shoe and hoof.

The view from the kitchen window.

If your property has not yet been fenced, then all your options are open—and, of course, the best ones (V-mesh woven wire, four-board poly fencing, etc.) are the most expensive. Whatever you choose to install, continue to board the horse until your fencing, shelter, water, and pasture are truly ready for your horse.

Make Your Pastures Horse-Safe

Call your County Extension agent and ask him to come out and check your pastures. Do you know what's growing there? Are you sure? You'll need to know before you let a horse graze there. Horses are much more delicate than cows, digestively speaking, and some plants are toxic to them. If the pretty tree in or near your pasture is a red maple, for instance, don't bring the horse home until you've had the tree removed. Wilted leaves from a red maple will cause

The view from the living-room window.

BOOKS

Complete Plans for Building Horse Barns Large and Small
by Nancy W. Ambrosiano and Mary F. Harcourt

Read this before you build your barn or indoor arena. This useful book, now in its second edition, gives you advice on barn selection and on working with builders. It also provides information on arena design, footing, lighting, ventilation, water, fencing, and stall design.

fatal liver failure in horses. There is no antidote and no cure.

Put Up a Shelter

Your horse will need some kind of a shelter, even if it's just a three-sided shed facing away from the prevailing wind direction. Find out what's involved in putting up a shelter and fencing, and then talk to your child again, just to be sure that you understand one another. If your idea of bringing the horse home involves a shed and a fence, and her idea involves a four-stall barn with a washrack, tack room, heat, lights, hot and cold running water, and an attached indoor arena, you may not be, as the saying goes, "on the same page."

Buy Basic Equipment

If you do have the same things in mind, then go ahead and purchase your equipment. All the things that your child took for granted at the boarding barn will need to be purchased by you. You'll need buckets, more buckets, and feed tubs; a wheelbarrow, a manure fork, a rake, a broom; halters and leadropes—and safety halters with breakaway crownpieces if you plan to turn out horses wearing halters. Your daughter probably already has a complete grooming kit, but now she and you will need a first-aid kit for human and another one for equines. And if your child will be doing a great deal of riding at home, you should invest in a few books that will help her keep up her skills.

Q & A

Q: *My children are both in college now, and I'm keeping their horses for them. We are lucky to have a farm where we can keep them, and my husband and I both like the horses and have no trouble handling them. But I'd love to save a little money while the kids are away at college, so I'm thinking that it might be okay to have them shod less often since they aren't being ridden, maybe every twelve weeks instead of every eight weeks.*

A: You're on the right track. You can probably save money on shoeing, but not by lengthening the intervals to twelve weeks. Horses should have their hooves trimmed every five to eight weeks whether or not they are shod and whether or not they were working. As their hooves grow, the growth isn't perfectly even, and over time, the hooves become unbalanced and the hoof-pastern axis is no longer straight. A trim every five to eight weeks will keep the hooves in balance and help the horses stay sound.

Talk to your kids and to the farrier. If the horses have ordinary shoes—that is to say, not special therapeutic shoes to alleviate the pain of a chronic lameness or disease—then it should be a simple matter to remove them. The horses could then go barefoot, which is good for their feet, and you would pay much less for trimming than for shoeing. Your farrier won't mind this—farriers invariably have much more work than they can handle, and they are not interested in doing work that isn't actually needed. Your farrier is usually the first, not the last, to tell you that your horse can do well without special shoes, pads, or any shoes at all.

Q: *We brought our daughter's horse to our new "farmette" a few months ago, to join my husband's old retired roping horse. They get along just fine, and we haven't had any problems. Now we're going away for a few days, and we hope this won't be a problem. The horses live in the pasture, they have a shed they can walk into if the weather gets rough, there's a big automatic water tank, and we'll throw a lot of extra hay over the fence before we leave. My daughter is having a fit about this and saying that she has to stay with the horses, that we can't leave them on their own, etc. She is ten, and she certainly won't be staying; she is going with us. But I'd like to know what to say to her so that she'll understand that a few days away just isn't a big deal.*

A: I can completely understand your need to get away for a day or two, but even if you can't or don't choose to have someone live in your house and "horse-sit," at least arrange to have someone drop by and check your horses twice a day. Your daughter is right in this case—horses shouldn't be left alone with no one checking on them. It's the downside of having your horses at home, and it's the reason that people who travel a lot often choose to board their horses elsewhere instead of keeping them at home.

Q: *We're getting ready to bring my daughter's horse home. The place is completely ready, we've been working on it for almost two years. There's a little barn, a riding arena, and a pasture with a run-in shed. All the fencing is horse safe. But before we bring Banner home, we need to know one more thing. Will he miss his buddies?*

At the boarding barn, he is turned out in a paddock with two other horses, but they don't seem to be very close friends. But we've heard from other people that horses shouldn't be kept alone. My daughter says that she's his best friend, so he won't need another horse to "talk to." Is she right? We can't afford to buy another expensive horse. Would a goat do?

A: Horses do need companionship. They are highly social, gregarious herd animals, and they usually don't do well alone. This doesn't mean that you have to buy an expensive horse, though. You may be able to provide Banner with a companion by accepting a retired horse that needs to live out his days in a pasture. Many owners keep their horses until they die of old age, and such owners are always on the lookout for the perfect retirement home.

A retired racehorse would be another possibility—Thoroughbreds and Standardbreds can be adopted from racehorse "recycling" centers. And you could give Banner company and do a good deed by adopting a horse or pony from a rescue organization; many rescued animals cannot be ridden or can be ridden only lightly, but all would appreciate the kind of home you've created. If it's not possible to find a suitable horse or pony, then a goat may do.

If your family is very experienced with horses and horse-training, you could also look into the possibility of adopting a mustang from The Bureau of Land Management (BLM).

Getting There and Back

If your horse lives at the boarding barn and can travel to shows in the barn's trailer behind the barn's truck, with stable staff along to load and unload horses and equipment, you're lucky. Most trailering tends to be a do-it-yourself proposition, and yours will be too if you keep your horse at home.

TRAILERING HORSES SAFELY

Trailering may also become a DIY proposition even if you stay at that boarding barn. Barn trailers tend to go to certain shows and not others, and they tend to go with a full load of horses or not at all. If your

B O O K S

Trailer-Loading Success by Diane Longanecker

This is a book about how to get the horse into the trailer. With it's help, you will learn a simple, step-by-step process to train your horse to load calmly. Each step is illustrated with drawings and photographs, and two case studies document training a young horse to load for the first time and retraining an older, problem horse.

Trailer-loading, like anything else taught to a horse, cannot be rushed. It must be taught safely, slowly, and systematically. This book will help you learn to do exactly that. The author has included a preloading checklist and a large number of safety tips.

child begins to go to quite a few shows, wants to go to a different kind of show, or takes an interest in trail-riding or off-property clinics, you will need to borrow or buy the means of transport, and learn how to handle them.

Practice at Home First

Before you ever take a horse anywhere in a trailer, practice preparing, loading, and unloading the horse. Practice hooking up your trailer and then practice driving, stopping, turning, changing lanes, and—oh dear—backing the trailer. Then put the horse in the trailer and practice it all again. Do everything in your power to make

Like everything else to do with horses, trailering requires equipment, training, and preparation.

yourself, your child, and your horse ready so that at least this part of the trailering experience will be comfortable and familiar.

Check the Specs Before You Tow

You may need a new vehicle for towing purposes—not all vehicles can pull trailers safely. Before you attach a trailer of any size to your truck or van, learn the answers to these questions:

1. What is the towing capacity of your vehicle?
2. If you add the weight of your trailer and horse(s), the weight of the equipment in the trailer, and the weight of the equipment and people in the vehicle, do you still have a comfortable margin for safety?
3. Is your engine powerful enough to handle the weight of the trailer and horses? Will it be powerful enough to handle the trailer on hills and in mud?
4. Is your vehicle equipped with a heavy-duty transmission—and a transmission cooler?
5. Is your vehicle equipped with good brakes in good condition?
6. Are the tires on both the towing vehicle and the trailer in good shape?
7. Is your vehicle equipped with a strong, solid, top-rated hitch? "Bumper pull" trailers are not attached to the bumper, and you should never even consider towing a trailer from a hitch that is attached to the bumper. The hitch must be firmly attached to the frame of the vehicle, and the ball must be of a suitable size to handle your trailer.

You May Need a New Tow Vehicle

If you are thinking of purchasing a vehicle that can pull a trailer, look at the largest, longest, heaviest ones. Most SUVs are not suited to trailer-pulling. A large pickup truck with a long wheelbase, a heavy van, or a Suburban—the ultimate towing vehicle—will be the most likely to take all the work in stride. Even if your child's first horse is small, think big from the beginning—it may save you trouble if you're easily able to pull a larger trailer than your current one and larger horses than the ones you are hauling now. If your child wants to travel to shows with another child and her horse, both horses must be able to fit into your trailer. And if a day comes when your own child gets a second, larger horse, you won't be faced with the need to buy another trailer as well.

H O R S E S E N S E

Safety-Check Your Trailer

Whether you are the handy sort who likes to do this or whether you take your trailer to a reliable mechanic to have the check done, never begin your trailering season without checking that all is well with your horse's home on wheels.

Even if you're very busy and wearing good clothing, you can perform some of the checks yourself, quite easily, without getting dirty. Look at your state regulations for trailers, and be sure that you are in compliance. Check that your lights are all intact and functioning: brake lights, running lights, turn signals, and emergency flashers.

Then turn the trailer over to a mechanic. A good mechanic will check everything: bearings and seals, brakes and pads, tire condition and pressure. He will check the state of the trailer flooring, and that of the trailer frame and undercarriage: rotted wood, rusty metal, and structural stress/damage must all be identified and repaired before that first trip. He will also check for rust—and fix and repaint rusty areas if you ask.

Be sure that you carry an emergency kit in your trailer or towing vehicle. This will be similar to the one you probably already carry in your car: jumper cables, jack, flares, "Emergency—Call Police" signs, duct tape, electrical tape, WD-40, a flashlight.

Q & A

Q: I'm taking my son and daughter and two of their friends to a horse show. It's the first time I'll have done this since we bought our own truck and trailer; before this we've always gone with the kids' instructor. She'll meet us at lunch, but I'm a little bit nervous about trying to organize kids, horses, stalls, bedding, numbers, and everything else, and I'm worried that I'll get there and see all four kids disappear in different directions while I try to cope with it all.

A: My prescription would be four clipboards, four pens, and four lists—let the kids help out! Give them their assignments before you leave, discuss the details in the car, and you'll be much better able to cope when you arrive at the show.

One person can sign in and pick up the show packets, get a copy of the schedule, set his or her watch to official show time,

B O O K S

Essential Reading on the Road

Whenever you take your horses anywhere in a trailer, carry these two small books: "The Hawkins Guide to Horse Trailering on the Road" and "The Hawkins Guide to Equine Emergencies on the Road." These little booklets will fit neatly into the glove box of your towing vehicle, and you should never leave home without them.

With these reference guides and a cell phone, you'll be equipped to deal with almost any situation that may arise: If you need a stable for the night or a towing service that can handle trucks and trailers, the information will be at your fingertips. If your horse becomes ill or injured on the road, you'll have information that will help you reach a nearby equine veterinarian and cope until he arrives.

and bring the packets and schedule back to the stabling area, where everyone will then synchronize their watches.

One person can locate the stalls and check that they are bedded or that bedding is available. Someone else can hang and fill the water buckets. The fourth person can unload each horse and lead it into its stall, while you stay with the truck and trailer. When the horses are in their stalls, everyone should come out and take all the equipment out of the truck and trailer so that you can move onto the parking area, and let the truck and trailer behind you move up and unload. You'll have to figure out your schedule and assignments based on what you know about the show and the kids—but this should get you off to a good start.

CHAPTER 15

Show Manners: Yours and Your Child's

Your child, your child's instructor, and the showbill will have prepared you for the show itself. All I can add is this: Stay out of the way and help when you're asked. Don't abandon your child to her own devices, but don't hover in an obvious way. If possible, at least at this first show, remain in the background unless she wants you right there with her.

HOW SHOULD I BEHAVE AT THE SHOW?

This is her own realm, and although she appreciates your support, she is more likely to get over her nerves on her own or with her peers and her instructor. If she is a teenager, she is likely to interpret your hovering as an implied criticism of her skills or of her instructor's ability.

If you watch and find that you have particular questions or concerns about your child's performance or attitude, don't bring them up at the show, and don't bring them up with the child. Write them down in a notebook and plan to discuss them later with the instructor. If you have questions or concerns about the coaching your child received at the show, do the same thing.

WHEN CAN WE LEAVE?

It's fine to start packing up and cleaning up as soon as your child's last class is over, and everyone is always eager to get back to the barn, put the horses away, and go home for that long-awaited shower and comfy chair. But there's a certain etiquette about showing, and if possible, whether or not you're expecting ribbons, try to stay for the awards (usually the last event of the day) before you leave.

After the show, let the child tell you about it. Don't be in a hurry to leap in with congratulations or sympathy. Find out how she feels about the experience. You may find that she is annoyed with herself for a poor ride that won a ribbon or that she is delighted by an accomplishment that wasn't reflected in the placings. Let her tell you what her perceptions and conclusions are. If she rode well and did her best, then, "Honey, I'm so proud of you" will be perfectly appropriate, regardless of the official results.

This will also be a time for you to learn what your child's focus is. "It isn't whether you win or lose, it's how you play the game" is a wonderful attitude to inculcate in children. Your child cannot always win—but she can always do her best, and if both you and she value this, then she will be happy much more often than she will be if winning and happiness are synonymous.

If you find that her focus is on winning rather than on effort, sportsmanship, or horsemanship, you will need to talk with her, and with her instructor, although not necessarily at the same time.

Help her focus on the quality of her own effort, of beating her previous performance, rather than on the quality of the judging or on the importance of beating other riders.

At shows, be discreet with praise and sympathy. A smile and wave will acknowledge a good performance, but if matters don't go so well, you'll have to know when to pull back and offer silent support. A

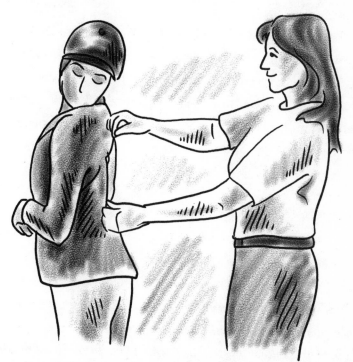

Parents have their uses on show day. Always bring safety pins and your sense of humor.

smile, a pat, a sigh of sympathy may be all that's needed. Don't feel that you have to explain or fix matters—you probably can't anyway, and it may not be appropriate for you to try.

Before you congratulate or sympathize too overtly, be certain that you understand why your child likes shows and what she wants to achieve. Her ambitions may not be yours, and vice versa. You may not give a rap about ribbons, and she may be obsessed with them— and in that case, saying "Oh, pish, it's just a silly strip of nylon!" will cause her to roll her eyes and write you off as a totally uncompre-hending adult.

Alternatively, your child may be the most talented little rider since the beginning of time, ideally suited for the show ring in your opinion, but utterly lacking in the ambitions that you believe you would have in her position.

Don't try to make your ambitions your child's ambitions. If you want to win ribbons at shows, take lessons yourself, compete, and enjoy it. A shared interest in horses can bring you and your child together, but only if you understand your child. Learn why she wants to ride and what it means to her; find out what she gets out of it, what she likes most about it, and what her ambition and desires are.

Q & A

Q: When I'm at a horse show with my daughter, what should I do when the judging is obviously unfair? I know that it's wrong to make a big fuss, and I certainly would never scream or yell the way some mothers do, but I believe that it just isn't right to see my child leave the ring disappointed when she should have placed higher.

A: You should do nothing at all, for several reasons. First, you might be wrong about the judging. Another rider may have made a mistake when you saw it and the judge didn't see it; your daughter may have made a mistake when you didn't see it and the judge did.

At home, find out how your daughter's day went and how she rode. Put the emphasis where it belongs, on the quality of the riding, not on the color of the ribbon.

If you are certain that you are correct and the judge was wrong, then write it off as a bad moment and go on with your lives. Judges are human. They blink and cough and get dust in their eyes; they get tired. They're judging large classes, and no matter how hard they try, they can't possibly observe every single movement that every single horse and rider make in a class. Most judges try hard to be fair and to do their best, which is all a judge—or a rider, horse, or parent—can do. If a particular judge is consistently unfair, then "vote with your feet" and don't participate in competitions when that judge is in the box.

Don't be too quick to complain to or sympathize with your daughter about the unfairness of it all. Your daughter can learn two very valuable lessons from these moments. One lesson is that life is not fair, and sometimes we don't get what we deserve. The other lesson is that life has both swings and roundabouts. If she competes often enough, there will be times when she doesn't get a ribbon that she deserved. If she competes often enough, there will also be times when she will get a ribbon that she didn't deserve. Either way, the ribbon can't be the reason that she rides. What you can do is encourage her to keep her perspective. Once again, put the emphasis where it belongs—on the horse, the ride, the skill, the sport, and the life lessons that riding and competing can provide.

Q: I took my daughter to a show last week, and it was the best show I've ever been to. I've attended enough of these now to know a little bit about them, and this one was amazing. It ran on time, there was enough parking, enough stabling, and free ice water all over the place, which was very much appreciated by us moms and dads. The whole thing ran very smoothly. It's the only show she's been to in three years that was like this—how can we find more shows like this? I wouldn't even mind being on a show-organizing committee if we could put together a show like this one.

A: The first thing you should do is send a letter to the organizers of that show and tell them exactly what you've told me. People who fall short of expectations need to be told, so that they can do better, and people who meet or exceed expectations need to be told, so that they know their efforts have been noticed and appreciated.

The second thing you can do is to write down every single thing you liked about this show and why it was different from previous shows. No detail is too small to note. At this point, you have the beginning of a show-organizer's plan.

Third, talk to people involved with local shows, and ask if you can be involved. You may not be invited to participate on an organizer's committee right away, but on the other hand, you may be. And either way, you'll be learning more about shows and show organization.

Fourth, when you feel confident enough, talk to the owner of your daughter's barn and ask whether he would be interested in holding a small show on the premises. If the answer is "Yes," then you'll have a chance to start planning a show of your own.

CHAPTER 16
Time for a Change

You've just bought your first horse—but it's never too soon to begin considering your child's future needs. One disadvantage of beginning riding as a child is that it's not uncommon for a young rider to outgrow a horse.

CHANGING HORSES: MOVING UP

Outgrowing can be literal: your tiny ten-year-old grows a foot taller in the next four years, and can't jump her pony anymore because her feet hang so far below the pony's belly that they catch the jumps and knock them down.

Outgrowing can also be metaphorical: it can mean that five years on, the kindly fifteen-year-old gelding who taught your child to ride and jump is now twenty and slowing down. He simply can't canter as fast as he used to or jump as high as he once did, and he would do better to drop back a level or two and canter small jumps with a new child rider. Meanwhile, your child needs to move up a level with a younger, stronger horse that can gallop a cross-country course and jump larger and more demanding fences.

It should be simple—after all, getting a new horse and selling this one is what's best for the horse and for your child. But there are emotional issues involved, and it can be terribly hard for a child to admit "I want a new horse; I want to move up; Prince can't do what I want to do, and it's not fair to ask it of him." And it's even harder for that child to agree to sell a beloved horse.

Sometimes we have to face the fact that a child has outgrown a horse . . .

Help Your Child Achieve Priority

So what's a parent to do? You have a situation that is difficult for parents: Your child has to make a decision that will take her down one path or another, and your job is to make it clear that a decision must be made—and then to sit quietly and not overwhelm your child with helpful advice. When the decision has been made, it will be time for you to offer suggestions, but not until then. What you can do, however, is help your child figure out her own priorities and ambitions.

If she enjoys riding because it's fun and it allows her to spend time with her beloved horse, then Prince is unlikely to be sold, and you would be wrong to press her to sell him and buy a horse to fulfill ambitions that aren't hers.

But that outgrown animal may be the perfect size for someone else!

But if she desperately wants to move her own riding to a higher level, to push the limits of her own abilities, and she knows that she can't do these things with Prince, but she feels guilty and disloyal when she admits this to herself, then Prince should either be retired to pasture and visited regularly, or sold or leased to a child who needs exactly the sort of horse that Prince is now.

This option, by the way, is one great advantage of belonging to Pony Club—good, solid, reliable horses suitable for beginners are always in demand, and many a good, solid, reliable horse has passed from one young Pony Clubber to another, teaching youngster after youngster to ride, and then returned to his original owner as a pampered retiree.

Sometimes, though, a second horse is needed for a much sadder reason—the death, through illness, misadventure, or age, of your child's first horse.

Q & A

Q: Our daughter's instructor is helping us right now, as we are trying to sell my daughter's horse (she has outgrown it) and look for a new horse. My daughter would like to sell the horse to someone local so that she can visit him and would really prefer to sell him to someone who boards at the same barn. Janice (the instructor) keeps saying, "That's a big mistake, don't do it, the best thing is to sell it out of state." This is a nice horse, and her saying that hurts my feelings. My daughter has done everything for her horse ever since we bought him, she's very particular about everything to do with him, and she won't stop caring about him even after he is sold; she's just not that kind of girl. What do you think?

A: I think that your instructor is probably right. You said it yourself: Your daughter has been in complete control of her horse's situation and handling ever since you bought him, and she has a certain way of doing everything. This can cause problems if the horse is sold to someone nearby.

In theory, it's nice to be able to pass a horse along to a friend or local acquaintance, because the old owner can help the new owner. In practice, this often doesn't work out at all. It can create a situation that will be desperately frustrating for your daughter, since the horse's new owner will almost certainly not do everything in the exact same way your daughter did. It will also be desperately frustrating for the horse's new owner, who won't appreciate being told how his new horse ought to be handled, tacked up, talked to, etc.

If you find a good home for your daughter's horse, let her have a day with the new owner, if that's something the new owner wants. During that day, your daughter will be able to explain and demonstrate everything she thinks the new owner will need to know and do—and after that, she should relax, accept that the horse is now someone else's, and focus on the search for her new horse.

Your instructor may be concerned that your daughter won't be able to focus on her new horse and her riding if she is constantly preoccupied with all the things that the other horse's new owner is doing "wrong"—even if "wrong" just means "not exactly the same way." It's hard to learn to let go, and it's harder for some people than it is for others. If it's particularly hard for your daughter, then "selling out of state" may not be such a bad idea after all, whether you take this as a literal suggestion or as a metaphor.

Q: *My fourteen-year-old daughter, Emily, has reached a point where she really needs to sell her horse and get one that can do the things she wants to do. She understands that, but she feels guilty about getting a new horse. She's driving me nuts going back and forth over this. One day she's desperate for a new horses, the next day she's crying because she thinks that she is being "unfaithful" to her old horse by even thinking about selling him.*

I can't afford to board two horses for her at $475 a month per horse. If she wants that other horse, Poco will have to go. If she doesn't get the other horse, she can't do what she wants at the shows. It doesn't seem that complicated to me, but then what do I know, I'm just Mom. I feel bad about pushing her for a decision, but time matters. I've already asked about a couple of horses that sound pretty good, and we need to plan shows for next year and get an ad into the paper to sell Poco.

A: Part of Emily's problem may be her age: The decision to let your first horse go is a difficult one at any age, but everything is difficult at fourteen, and this sort of decision may be impossible for her right now.

Part of the problem may also be that she simply doesn't know what her priorities are: If what matters most to her is her relationship with her horse, she'll want to keep Poco. If what matters most is moving ahead and doing well at the shows, she'll need to sell him. It sounds to me as though she isn't sure what she wants.

Why not leave her alone and not push for a decision? There's really nothing complicated involved at this point: She has a horse, she likes her horse, and she's considering the possibility of selling this horse and getting another one. Let her sort through her options and preferences on her own.

Whatever happens in the next year or two—and since she's just fourteen, there's no huge hurry—needs to happen because Emily made a decision, not because Emily went along with someone else's decision. The consequences of her decision, whenever she makes it, will belong to her, so why not allow her to have the responsibility and authority to make that decision for herself?

You obviously have great hopes for Emily in the showring, and there's nothing wrong with that, but it may not be her own first priority. Let her have the time she needs to think and consider. After all, she's not saying "Buy me the second horse and let me keep them both until I decide which one to keep"; she's saying "Don't force me to make a decision right now." It's not an unreasonable request.

She may make the wrong choice, or the choice that seems wrong to you, but it will be her choice, and the process of making choices and living with the consequences is a big part of growing up. And you'll be there to help her if she asks and to catch her if she falls—standing back and letting her grow doesn't mean that you are abandoning your child, only that you are letting her become an independent individual in her own right.

Til Death Us Do Part

CHAPTER 17

Losing a horse can affect a child much more profoundly than losing a human relative. Some parents are shocked by this—other, wiser parents understand.

LOSING A HORSE: A DEATH IN THE FAMILY

To a child, that horse represented unconditional acceptance. Children spend hours talking to their horses and "just hanging out" with them, at a time when nobody else in their lives has that much time to listen to them. The horse is their playmate, their soul mate, and many children, when asked, "Who is your best friend?," will automatically, and truthfully, say the name of their horse. If you understand the importance of the horse in your child's life, you'll be able to understand and deal with your child's reactions and emotions on the death of that horse.

Deal With Anger

One of the first feelings children of any age will feel is anger—their horse left them, and they feel the same sense of being abandoned that they would feel if they lost a family member. Depending on your child's age and personality, you may find that your normally sweet child is distant and distracted and tends to snap at you—or you may find that your normally busy, preoccupied, fiercely independent child is suddenly lethargic and clinging. Children in this situation are experiencing loss, grief, anger, and one more damaging, dangerous emotion: guilt.

Deal With Guilt

Guilt is something that adults struggle with—but it's even more difficult for children, because children lack an adult frame of reference. Children's guilt is disproportionate, inappropriate, out of context—because a child took so much pride in being responsible for her horse's care, she will feel an equal amount of guilt when he dies or is euthanized. After all, *responsible* means responsible for everything about her horse, and thus, to her, it's clear that she was somehow responsible for his death. You will need to explain, patiently and probably often, that nothing your child did or neglected to do caused the horse to die.

Explain What Death Is

If your child is a preschooler, it won't be easy to explain death, because for most preschoolers, the concept is incomprehensible. *Asleep, taking a nap, lying down,* and *dead* are all the same to a preschooler, and your young child may go on expecting to see the horse again at any moment.

By the time your child reaches kindergarten, and for the next five years or so, the concept of *death* exists, and the child may even recognize the finality of it—but will also agonize about how the death could have been avoided or prevented. This is where the guilt will come into the picture, and you will need to explain, again and again, that the death was not avoidable and was not the child's fault.

Deal With Depression

Children of eleven or twelve can become desperately unhappy and depressed when they lose a horse or another beloved animal; this is the age at which they will typically refer to the horse as their "best friend"—and mean it. The best thing you can do for children at this age is to encourage them to talk about and express their feelings for their dead friend. The next best thing you can do for them is to keep them away, as much as possible, from the unthinking unkindness of adults who try to be "helpful" by saying, "For heaven's sake, it was just a horse!" There's no such thing as "just" a horse.

Teenagers are likely to become withdrawn and hide in their rooms, doing their mourning privately or on the telephone with friends, behaving as though they don't care, and brushing off any parental attempts at comfort. They do care, very much, but they're internalizing their anguish in typical adolescent fashion.

Don't take the apparent rejection personally—there's no room in their minds for the notion that you might be upset too, by the horse's death, by their pain, or by both. And don't enforce the telephone time limits for a few months—teens will usually get a good deal of their support from other teens, especially those who have the same sort of feelings about their horses.

Give your teenager time. Be patient, keep telling yourself, "And this too shall pass," talk to your teen if talking is appropriate, but don't bang on the bedroom door and demand to discuss it or say "It's time to move on." And above all, don't begin a conversation about buying a new horse—wait. You'll know when the time is right, because your child will know, and the subject will be brought up by her.

R E S O U R C E S

For Dealing with Grief

If you need help dealing with a child who is dealing with the loss of a horse, or if you feel that your child would be more willing to accept help from someone outside the family, that help is only a phone call away. There are several hotlines available for those grieving over the loss of an animal; many are sponsored by universities well known for their veterinary schools and equine research programs.

Chicago Veterinary Medical Association: (708) 603-3994
Michigan State University: (517) 432-2696
Tufts University: (508) 839-7966
University of California at Davis: (916) 752-4200.

You might also visit the local library or bookstore and look for helpful items such as:

The Loss of a Pet by Wallace Sife
Coping with Sorrow on the Loss of Your Pet by Moria Anderson

Q & A

Q: *We're ready to buy my daughter a pony, and we've found one that we love and her instructor loves and even our Pony Club DC loves! There's just one problem: this pony is twenty-one years old. From what I understand, that's really old for a horse. Is it realistic to think that this one will still be rideable for a few years before it retires? The vet says that it is sound for riding and wouldn't be too stressed by the work it would get (my daughter is a D-1). I'm worried about two things: how long this pony will be useful, and then what will happen when he dies? Kathy is only nine years old, and I wouldn't want her to fall in love with this pony and then have it die in a year or two.*

A: I don't think you have much to worry about. Ponies are durable beasts; many ponies continue under saddle into their late twenties. Many ponies have taught several generations of a family to ride. Some ponies don't retire from active duty until they are well over thirty.

A healthy, sound, active pony can go on and on if it's treated and managed correctly.

Could it die in a year or two? Certainly—but so could the three-year-old horse in the next stall. And the main killer of horses—colic—isn't age-related. I'd say that a solid, sturdy, sound, and healthy twenty-one-year-old pony would be a good bet. Your biggest problem may be figuring out what to do with him in ten years when your daughter leaves for college.

Q: *My son's horse had to be put down a month ago. He's still moping about it. I've told him that I'll buy him another horse, but he says he doesn't know if he wants to ride anymore. We had given him three years of lessons, and he was riding a lot and winning a lot, and I'm*

disappointed that he's willing to throw all of that investment away.
What can I do to get him back on track?

A: Your son is mourning for his beloved companion and friend. He needs to be given time to mourn, and a month isn't very long. It's wonderful that you're willing to buy him another horse, but he knows that the offer has been made—now you should leave that subject alone and let him bring it up when he's ready.

Instead of trying to get your son to look at horses, spend time with him without talking about horses, unless he starts the discussion himself. Take him to a movie or to a car show or to an art show. Put up the basketball hoop and go one-on-one. Play catch. If you can't shoot or pitch, never mind—go for a walk with him. Show him, through your actions, that you love him, that you are proud of him (not just of the ribbons he won), and that you are, as the current phrase says, "there for him." It's entirely possible that the word "horse" won't ever come up, but your son will know that you love him.

I understand that you are proud of your son and proud of the fact that he won a lot, but don't be concerned about your investment. It's quite safe. If you think about it, you'll realize that you were investing in your son, not in the sport or the competitions or those trophies and ribbons. You wanted to provide your son with a great opportunity, and you did. Your investment was in him, and he isn't throwing anything away.

Those three years of lessons weren't wasted. Your son learned new skills, he participated in a sport—and very successfully, too. He could return to riding next week, next month, next year, in four years or ten years or never, and he would still have the benefits of what he learned in those three years. Riders learn much more than riding skills. They learn patience, tolerance, and how to look out for the interests, health, and happiness of another being. It doesn't matter that the being is of another species—the experience made your son a better person, and that won't change just because his horse has died. Your son will be a better friend, a better employee (or employer), and a better husband and parent because of what he's learned from his three years with his horse. I'd say that you made a very good investment indeed.

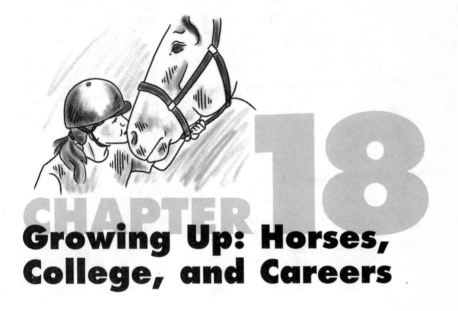

CHAPTER 18
Growing Up: Horses, College, and Careers

It's a familiar scenario: the soon-to-be high-school graduate asks for a family meeting and then drops a bomb—she wants to take a year off to be a working student for some famous rider, she wants to take a year off before college to study for her Pony Club "A" rating, or she wants to go to college . . . and major in Riding. What's a parent to do?

MY CHILD WANTS TO WORK WITH HORSES!

The best thing to do is nothing—at least until you've done some homework on the subject. Don't overreact, no matter what your opinion may be. "Let's talk about that on the twenty-fourth; it's your father's day off, and we'll plan to make that *your* day" is a much more useful reaction than "Don't be silly; you're going to start college in the fall and major in Accounting."

Then use your time to do a lot of homework. Talk to your vet, to your child's instructor, and to any other professional you know in the horse world. Talk to the DC of the local Pony Club.

"I want a year to study for my 'A'!"

Taking a year off to study for the Pony Club "A" rating is actually reasonable and realistic; the amount and depth of information needed to achieve the rating is enough to warrant a year's study. There's a time limit—the upper age limit is twenty-one. College, on the other hand, may be started at any time. Unlike many other certificates from programs of dubious value, the Pony Club "A" carries the stamp of professional-level achievement, so it's an investment in her future with horses: If she ever wants to teach riding or to manage a barn, she should have no difficulty finding employment, and if she chooses to attend vet school, the "A" won't hurt her chances at all. And there's another advantage: That first year of college will be a breeze after the year of cramming for the "A" rating.

"I want to be a working student for Mr. Famous Rider!"

Taking a year to be a working student for a famous rider is another matter. This tends to work out better in theory than in practice; many working students go off with high hopes and large ambitions, imagining that they will do a lot of riding, take a lot of lessons, and be the "right-hand-man" of the famous rider. In fact, most of them find, to their chagrin, that they are there to clean stalls, roll bandages, groom horses, and scrub waterbuckets from dawn until well after dusk. The lessons may be few and far between—famous riders generally need to focus their energy on themselves and on any paying students, as well as on the owners of the horses they ride. And the lessons may also be unsatisfactory—many famous riders are dreadful teachers. Faced with constant fatigue and frustration, many of these working students quit and return home after a few months, a few weeks, or even a few days. It's a good idea to discourage this particular notion, unless your child knows for a fact that *this* famous rider is different or unless her interest is not in riding, but in learning how a famous rider's barn is run.

"I do want to go to college this fall, but I want to major in Riding!"

This may not be as bad as it sounds. Again, do your homework. What you learn now will help you deal with the would-be working student, as well. At least your child wants to go to college!

The sad fact is that the world is not crowded with brilliant opportunities for graduates of Equine Studies programs; the sad fact is that the world is *not* full of famous riders looking for eager young working students to mentor. It is a fact that only a very few people in the horse world make money by riding. It's also a fact that the people who make money in the horse industry are generally not people who have much time to spend riding.

Reality and the Horse Industry Riding is rather like golf in that it makes money for a few players and takes money from most players. The majority of the people who make money in golf derive their income from peripheral activities: not from playing, but from sales, accounting, advertising. Some make money from designing or producing clothing, golf clubs, and golf carts—and some make money working for the people who design or produce those things. The horse world is very similar. Here, too, there are very few people who are paid to ride. Most riders pay for the privilege of riding, and the only real question is what they will do in "real life" to make the money that will allow them to afford to pursue their chosen hobby.

Those Working in the Horse Industry Usually Can't Find Time to Ride

It's a peculiar paradox that those individuals who spend their lives and make their income working in the horse industry—teachers, trainers, barn owners, veterinarians, farriers—are frequently unable to find the time to ride. Whether the job in question involves a boarding barn, a teaching stable, or a tackshop, there are a few constant factors: the work is hard, the hours are long, and the money isn't always good. There *are* people who have the time to ride and the money to improve their riding skills through lessons and clinics; they also have the time to read books and watch videotapes to improve their understanding of their particular discipline and the money to purchase those items. But in almost every case, the people with the time and money to ride and enjoy their horses are the people who have found other ways to assure themselves of a steady, adequate income.

College Career and Horses—Your Child Can Have It All

Many young riders don't understand that studying something worthwhile, interesting, and potentially lucrative does not mean abandoning horses. On the contrary, it may be the single course of action that will make it possible for those riders to go on riding for the rest of their lives.

Another idea that young riders should understand is that it will be entirely possible for them to create or find horse-related work no matter what their college course of study may be. Large horse farms and horse businesses need accountants and people to design their brochures and sales catalogues. Pharmaceutical companies need doctors and pharmacists and research scientists to develop new medicines for horses. Feed companies need researchers, nutritionists, and writers who can popularize what they do. Tack and clothing must be made, shown, sold to retailers, shipped, and sold again to customers. Doctors can specialize in sports medicine for riders; people who study chiropractic or massage therapy can take extra courses and apply those same skills to work on equines.

And the list goes on. Business, medicine, photography, law—all are subjects that can lead to careers in the equine industry. Not just some, but all the best and most highly regarded horse experts in the industry studied other subjects in college and even in graduate school.

Many colleges offer courses in Equine Studies.

RESOURCES

College Horse Homework

Instead of demanding that your college-bound child sign up for a more traditional college major, try treating her as a burgeoning adult who learns as adults—including you—learn. Give her information resources. Purchase a copy of Bonnie Kreitler's book *50 Careers With Horses*, and read it with her. This book offers information about a wide variety of careers in all parts of the equine industry, together with descriptions of the work involved, the salary range, related positions, and the college degree(s) that will lead most directly and easily to each career. She may develop a deep and abiding interest in a career that she had never heard of before reading the book—or she may simply choose to keep her options open and use her college years to discover new subjects and find new interests, which is one of the best uses of those years.

Q & A

Q: My daughter is trying to choose a college major, but insists that it has to have something to do with horses. I've always thought that she would major in something artistic, but she's talking about courses that would let her be a veterinarian's assistant or someone who runs a barn. I'm privately horrified but don't dare say that.

I can't think that she would stay with anything like those jobs; she's a very sensitive, artistic young lady (she could be an illustrator for a magazine if magazines still had drawings instead of photographs). I even suggested photography, because she is artistic, but she says it's not the same as drawing or painting, and she doesn't like looking through a lens.

A: Stop worrying, please. The first year or two of college courses are usually the same or nearly the same regardless of the student's major, because there are so many required courses. Your daughter will be able to change her major without much trouble.

Whatever she chooses today is something she can change tomorrow or in the next weeks or months. As she takes new classes, meets new people, and becomes exposed to new ideas, she may end up with a major in some subject she's not even heard of yet. If she makes a change very late in her college years, she might have to put in an extra semester to make up any specific required courses in the new subject, but that's not exactly a fate worse than death.

As for being artistic, that tendency could take her in any number of directions. Magazines may not use many drawings these days, but books certainly do—including this one. Authors and publishers of fiction and nonfiction are always looking for new, talented illustrators. On the academic side, medical and veterinary textbooks still require detailed illustrations, and someone has to create them.

Portraits of horses, drawn or painted, are increasingly popular among horse owners and provide a very lucrative income for the talented artists who can recreate a photograph in charcoal, pen and ink, or paint.

Horse art in all forms is popular—look at some copies of the magazine *Equine Images.* If your daughter wants to combine her love of horses and her artistic talent, there's no reason that she couldn't create a successful career out of that mixture.

Q: My daughter is eighteen and looking at colleges. I've driven her to about ten different ones, to look around, but she's not very interested in the academic side of things, she just wants to find a college where she can keep her horse either at the college or nearby. My husband and I would rather see her take a lot of different courses, learn new things, meet new people, and enjoy college. We're afraid that she'll spend all her time at the barn when she isn't in class or that she won't even go to class, because she's not all that interested in college anyway. What can we do?

A: You have two choices: first, you can send her to college without her horse. If she isn't interested in college, perhaps she shouldn't go at all—college isn't for everyone. But if she is interested enough to want to learn and do well, she will see the logic of leaving her horse in your good care while she goes off to experience four years that will be unlike any other four years of her life.

If her first year goes smoothly, her grades are good, her confidence is high, and she's spent some of her spare time finding a boarding stable that she likes somewhere near the school, then you can consider sending the horse back with her, perhaps on a semester-by-semester basis. If her work is too hard or her social life is too busy—both are quite common phenomena for college students—then the horse can go home again and wait for her in your pasture.

Second, you might consider not sending her to college. Your worry is well founded; it would be a shame for your daughter to go to college and spend all her time at the barn with her horse. She doesn't have to go to college to do that. It seems a bit like sending a younger child to camp and then finding out that she spent the entire summer in the cabin, reading the books that she brought from home. At camp, there are staff members whose job it is to ensure camper participation in activities; at college, unless it's a very small college, there's no one to serve that particular function.

You may need to remind your daughter that college is a privilege, not a right—and not a four-year holiday with her horse. And if a discussion about college ends with her stating that she doesn't see the point or doesn't want to go, offer her the chance to work for a year and then go to college. A year in the real world of entry-level employment can do a lot to correct a teenager's perspective about what college means.

CHAPTER 19

From Parent to Participant: Discovering Horses

The first effects may be subtle. In addition to the reverent quoting of anything her instructor has told her recently, your child will, at various times, proffer a tidbit of information about horses that will amaze and delight you: horses in history, horses in art, horses in nature, horses in movies. Your initial reaction will be pleasure in her pleasure and pleasure in the depth and breadth of her interest. You may find the time to sit down and watch a horsey movie or television program with her, and you'll be astonished and impressed at the intelligence of her occasional comments.

However, as her interest grows and she learns more and more

about horses and riding, you will no longer be able to sit down and enjoy watching a movie or television program together or at least not if there are horses on-screen. Occasional comments give way to a constant and critical commentary. Whenever a horse appears on-screen, your child will inform you what kind of horse it is, whether the tack is appropriate or not, whether the actor can ride or not, whether the situation is believable or not, and if you try to "Ssssshhhhhhh" your child, she will subside into the seat, sniff audibly, and say "That is SO bogus!" If you enjoy watching movies and television programs in peace, you may have to watch the horsey ones in your child's absence.

There may be times in your child's life when horses seem to be the only thing you still seem to have in common. Riding together and talking about horses can keep the communication lines open, and let you enjoy each other in spite of all your differences.

The fact that you are even considering watching horsey programs means that the process of conversion has begun. Like it or not, you are becoming something of a horsey parent. Even if you have been quite clear about your own lack of interest, fear of horses, and your strong dislike of large, unpredictable animals with hard feet, you will almost certainly find yourself pestered for a horse, for lessons, and for all that goes with that particular territory.

Later, you will find yourself driving to and watching horse shows and advising other parents on how to back a trailer. At some point, you may notice that it is part of your personal routine to pull out a rag and provide a last-minute wipedown to your child's boots before she enters the ring. Finally, at a moment when your defenses are low, you may find that your child has somehow persuaded you to go riding with her. This is a serious matter. Be warned: many a horse-obsessed adult rider began as the uninterested parent of a horse-obsessed child. But that's another story—and another book.

APPENDIX

GIFTS FOR YOUNG RIDERS

One hidden advantage to combining children and horses is this: From now on, neither you nor any of your relatives will ever have to wrack your brain figuring out what your child wants, needs, or might like. Horses provide many new opportunities to spend money.

Types of Gifts
- *Clothing:* breeches, boots, socks, leggings, gloves, vests, jackets, riding shirts, stock tie, stock pin. For older girls, sports bras make good gifts.
- *Tack and equipment:* saddle, bridle, bit, leathers, stirrups, reins, saddle pads—you can add another bit (perhaps a

pelham or kimblewicke, or whatever your instructor suggests). Other popular items: a tack trunk, a set of clippers, a leather halter with a nameplate, a stall nameplate, a grooming box, rags, fly bonnets, boots (for the horse).

➢ *Smaller gifts:* little things matter, too, and you can safely give brushes, hoofpicks, boot polish, mane and tail conditioner, spray bottles, saddle soap, leather conditioner, mane comb, pulling comb.

➢ *Educational gifts:* books, videotapes, magazine subscriptions, clinics (check with instructor before signing up your child for a clinic, so that you'll select the right clinician).

HORSE SENSE

Things That Riders Always Need

hoofpicks
gloves
socks
saddle soap
leadropes
horse treats
books about horses

When all else fails, or for relatives who might not find it so easy to visit a tackshop, every major catalogue and most tack shops offer gift certificates.

The most practical method is to hand the catalogues to the child and ask her to write in them, circling each desired item, marking size, color, and style, and designating each with one, two, or three stars depending on whether the item is, in her estimation, something that she would like to have, would really like to have, or need/wants desperately. Armed with those catalogues, you'll be sure that what is purchased is what the child truly wants.

RESOURCES FOR PARENTS

How Can I Learn More About Horses?

Taking riding lessons from your child's instructor may or may not be successful, for several reasons. For one, your child may find this embarrassing. For another, instructors differ, and you selected this one after going to a good deal of trouble to find a good teacher of children. That person won't necessarily be a good teacher of adults.

Horse-care lessons are another matter. Is there a large veterinary teaching hospital in your area? How about a college? Either or both may offer short courses in horse management. You may also be able to get useful information from your state horse council and from your cooperative extension horse specialist. If there is a horse-related lecture, seminar, clinic, or practicum in your area, these people should know about it.

And even if there are no hands-on opportunities, clinics, or lectures in your area, you can sit down with a good book: start with the *USPC Manual of Horsemanship* (volume 1).

RESOURCES

Helpful Telephone Numbers

American Horse Council
(202) 296-4031
American Horse
Shows Association
(212) 972-2472
American Medical
Equestrian Association
(502) 695-8940
National 4-H Council
(301) 961-2945
National Safety Council
(202) 293-2270
United States Combined
Training Association
(508) 887-9001
United States
Dressage Federation
(402) 434-8550
United States Pony Clubs, Inc.
(606) 254-7669

RADIO

Tune Your Radio to the Horse Show!

Horse radio is here—it's called "The Horse Show with Rick Lamb," and you can listen to interviews with well-known individuals from all parts of the equine industry. If the show isn't on the air in your home town, E-mail Rick@thehorseshow.com. He will tell you how to ask your stations to carry the show. In the meantime, you can hear interviews online by visiting the show's Web site:

http://www.thehorseshow.com/

Basic Books

There are thousands of horse books in bookstores and on library shelves—here are some of the most useful for your purposes. I've included books to help you understand horses, horse keeping and horse care, riding, rider psychology, and your child's particular discipline.

If you want to borrow these books from the library and your library doesn't have them, ask the library to purchase them—or request them via interlibrary loan.

If you want to purchase books but can't find them at the local tackshop or bookstore, you can ask either store to order books for you. Alternatively, you may wish to do some shopping online. Amazon.com is a wonderfully convenient source for books, including horse books. And don't forget to look for horse books at used book stores!

College and careers

50 Careers for Horses. Bonnie Kreitler

Health

Concise Guide to Colic in the Horse. David Ramey
Concise Guide to Nutrition in the Horse. David Ramey
Concise Guide to Medications and Supplements for the Horse. David Ramey

Horse Health Care. Cherry Hill

Dr. Kellon's Guide to First Aid for Horses. Eleanor Kellon

Equifacts: The Complete Horse Record Organizer. Russell Meerdink

Legal matters

Equine Law & Horse Sense. Julie Fershtman

Legal Forms, Contracts, and Advice for Horse Owners. Sue Ellen Marder

The Equine Legal Handbook. Gary Katz

Horse management

Horse Buyer's Notebook. Shawn McAfee

The Body Language of Horses. Tom Ainslie and Bonnie Ledbetter

Grooming to Win. Susan Harris

Horse Handling & Grooming. Cherry Hill

Horse keeping

Horsekeeping on a Small Acreage. Cherry Hill

The New Book of Saddlery and Tack. Carolyn Henderson

Rider psychology

Heads Up! Practical Sports Psychology for Riders, Their Trainers, and their Families. Janet Edgette

Riding

Learn Horseback Riding in a Weekend. Mary Gordon-Watson

Horse Gaits, Balance and Movement. Susan Harris

Riding for the Rest of Us: A Practical Guide for Adult Riders. Jessica Jahiel

Handbook of Riding Essentials. François Lemaire de Ruffieu

Happy Horsemanship. Dorothy Henderson Pinch

Training
Clicker Training for Your Horse. Alexandra Kurland
101 Arena Exercises. Cherry Hill

Trailers
The Complete Guide to Buying, Maintaining, and Servicing a Horse Trailer. Neva Kittrell Scheve
Hawkins Guide to Horse Trailering on the Road. Neva Kittrell Scheve
Hawkins Guide to Equine Emergencies on the Road. Neva Kittrell Scheve

Magazines for Young Riders
Stable Kids
P.O. Box 1802
Grand Island, NE 68802-1802

Young Equestrian
4905 Mexico Road
St. Peters, MO 63376

Young Rider
P.O. Box 725
Williamsburg, VA 23187-0725

Magazines for Teens and Up
Chronicle of the Horse
P.O. Box 46
Middleburg, VA 22117

Dressage Today
656 Quince Orchard Road
Gaithersburg, MD 20878-1472

Equus
656 Quince Orchard Road
Gaithersburg, MD 20878-1472

Horse Illustrated
P.O. Box 57549
Boulder, CO 80322-7549

Horse & Rider
12265 West Bayaud, Suite 300
Lakewood, CO 80228

Practical Horseman
6405 Flank Drive
Harrisburg, PA 17112

The Horse
P.O. Box 4710
Lexington, KY 40544-9945

Western Horseman
P.O. Box 7980
Colorado Springs, CO 80903-7980

Associations

American Association for Horsemanship Safety (AAHS)
Web site: http://www.law.utexas.edu/dawson/
(512) 488-2220

American Horse Shows Association (AHSA)
220 East 42nd Street
New York, NY 10017-5876
(212) 972-2472

American Medical Equestrian Association (AMEA)
4715 Switzer Road
Frankfort, KY 40601
(502) 695-8940
E-mail: dhammett@primeline.com

American Riding Instructor Certification Program (ARICP)
P.O. Box 282
Alton Bay, NH 03810
(603) 875-4000

American Youth Horse Council, Inc.
4093 Iron Works Pike
Lexington, KY 40511-2742
1-800-879-2942

CHA-The Association for Horsemanship Safety and Education
(CHA/AHSE)
5318 Old Bullard Road
Tyler, TX 75703
1-800-339-0138

Horsemanship Safety Association, Inc. (HSA)
517 Bear Road
Lake Placid, FL 33852-9726
(941) 465-0289

National 4-H Council
7100 Connecticut Avenue
Chevy Chase, MD 20815-4999
(301) 961-2959

United States Combined Training Association, Inc. (USCTA)
P.O. Box 2247
Leesburg, VA 22075
Web site: http://www.eventingusa.com/
E-mail: info@eventingusa.com
(703) 779-0440

United States Dressage Federation (USDF)
P.O. Box 6669
Lincoln, NE 68506
Web site: http://www.usdf.org/
E-mail: usdressage@navix.net
(402) 434-8550

United States Pony Clubs, Inc. (USPC)
4071 Iron Works Pike
Lexington, KY 40511-8462
Web site: http://www.ponyclub.org/
E-mail: ponyclub@gte.net
(606) 254-7669

Online Horse Resources

For those of you with Internet access, here are some of the best permanent Horse Sites on the World Wide Web:

Jessica Jahiel's Holistic Horsemanship:
http://www.prairienet.org/jjahiel

Jessica Jahiel's HORSE-SENSE E-mail Newsletter and Archives:
http://www.prairienet.org/horse-sense/

Kris Carroll's Horse Country and Junior Riders Digest:
http://www.horse-country.com/

The Horse Show with Rick Lamb: Radio for America's Horse Lovers
http://www.thehorseshow.com/

American Riding Instructors Association: Directory of Instructors
http://www.win.net/aria/

United States Pony Clubs, Inc.
http://www.uspc.org/index2.htm

Karen Pautz's HayNet: a guide to horse sites on the Internet
http://www.freerein.com/haynet/

Tack and Clothing

1824 Arnott Mason Corporation (plus-size clothing and footgear)
Web site: http://www.1824catalog.com
E-mail: info@1824catalog.com
(703) 818-1517

Boink (comfortable, all-weather clothing)
Web site: http://www.boinkcatalog.com
E-mail: info@boinkcatalog.com
1-800-471-4659

Dominion Saddlery (tack and clothing)
Web site: http://horsenet.com/dominion/
E-mail: dominion@horsenet.com
1-800-TACK UP

Dover Saddlery
Web site: http://doversaddlery.com
1-800-989-1500

Riding Right Catalog (clothing/equipment)
Web site: http://www.ridingright.com/
E-mail: requests@ridingright.com

Sergeant's Western World (western tack/clothing)
Web site: http://www.sergeantswestern.com/
1-800-333-3669

SuitAbility (patterns: make your own clothing)
Web site: http://www.SuitAbility.com/
E-mail: Linea@stormnet.com
1-800-207-0256

Tack In The Box (dressage)
Web site: http://www.tackinthebox.com/
E-mail: Pounce@tackinthebox.com
1-800-456-8225

Dressage Extensions (dressage)
Web site: http://www.Dressage-ext.com/
E-mail: DresExt@bbs.bbs-la.com
1-800-303-7849

Paul's Harness Shop (dressage, hunting, eventing, racing)
Web site: http://www.phssaddlery.com/
1-800-736-7285

Supplies for Horse and Barn

American Livestock Supply, Inc.
Web site: http://www.americanlivestock.com
E-mail: alshorse@itis.com
1-800-356-0700

United Vet Equine
Web site: http://www.unitedvetequine.com/
E-mail: info@unitedvetequine.com
1-800-328-6652

Valley Vet Supply
Web site: http://www.valleyvet.com/
E-mail: service@midusa.net
1-800-356-1005

GLOSSARY
EQUESTRIAN TERMS

Aged: means that the horse or pony is more than eight years old. You may see this term in a show program.

Aids: are used to direct the horse. The natural aids are the rider's legs, seat, voice, and hands; artificial aids are the spurs and whip.

Amateur: someone who is eighteen years or older and is not paid for riding horses or for any other work associated with horses.

American Horse Shows Association (AHSA): the national equestrian federation of the United States.

American Riding Instructor Certification Program (ARICP): a program that recognizes and certifies riding instructors who are proven to demonstrate competence, integrity, and safety.

Bell boots: protective boots that cover the horse's hooves.

Billets: straps under the flaps of English saddles; the billets attach to the girth buckles.

Blaze: a wide white stripe on a horse's face, running from forehead to nostrils.

Blemish: a cosmetically abnormal feature that doesn't affect a horse's soundness. White hairs from an old rub, a scar from a past injury, or a lump from a "cold" splint are blemishes—they look unsightly but don't diminish a horse's usefulness.

Bowed tendon: a damaged tendon in the horse's leg, behind the cannon bone, caused by stress.

Canter: a controlled gait of the horse, with three beats followed by a pause or moment of suspension during which the horse has all four feet off the ground.

Clean round: describes the completion of a prescribed course of jumps without time faults or jumping faults.

Coggins test: a blood test for diagnosing equine infectious anemia. Horse shows and most boarding barns will not allow a horse on the grounds until the horse's owner shows proof that the horse is free from this disease, by producing a copy of a current "Negative Coggins" test result.

Colic: the number one killer of horses, a painful digestive disturbance.

Color: there are hundreds of variations on horse coat color, but the basic ones are bay, chestnut, grey, and roan. Pinto horses are black and white (piebald) or brown and white (skewbald).

Colt: a young male horse under the age of four.

Combination: two or three obstacles set up to be jumped in quick succession, separated by one or two strides. A combination is considered to be a single obstacle. If a horse stops or runs out at any element of the combination, the entire obstacle must be rejumped.

Combined Training: also known as *eventing,* this sport is based on a test for cavalry horses and combines three tests of horse and rider: dressage, cross-country jumping, and show jumping.

Conformation: the physical structure, form, and type of body build of the horse.

Course: in each jumping class, competitors must negotiate the jumps in a prescribed order. Courses for each class are posted in advance.

Cross-bred: a horse with a sire of one breed and a dam of another. In writing, expressed with an *x*; for example, a Thoroughbred-Morgan cross would be designated "TBxMorgan."

Cross-ties: used to tie a horse in an aisle by fastening its halter to chains or ropes attached to rings set into opposite walls. Cross-ties should always be equipped with "panic snaps."

Curb: a curb bit features shanks and works off leverage, multiplying the effect of the rider's pressure on the reins. The mouthpiece of a curb bit may be straight, curved, ported, or it may feature one, two, or more joints.

Dam: the mother of a horse.

Deworming: sometimes referred to as *worming.* The regular administration of a deworming paste is necessary to maintain horses' health.

Most horses require deworming every six to eight weeks, year-round, so this is part of the regular expense of horse leasing or horse ownership.

Diagonals: at the trot, the rider will post (rise) on either the right or the left diagonal. On the right diagonal, she will rise as the horse's right foreleg reaches forward; on the left diagonal, she will rise as the horse's left foreleg reaches forward.

Disposition: one of the most important considerations when buying a horse. A kind, patient, generous disposition is essential in a child's horse.

Dressage: a classical system of educating and developing a horse so that he becomes strong, supple, balanced, and obedient.

Endurance riding: a sport of speed and endurance over distances.

Equitation: the art of riding.

Equitation classes: horse-show classes in which only the rider's skill is judged, not the quality or performance of the horse.

Farrier: a horse-shoer. Horses' hooves grow constantly, and the farrier trims the hooves regularly and shoes the horse if shoes are needed. You may not see this individual very often, but you will be writing a check to him every four to eight weeks, as long as you have a horse.

Federation Equestre Internationale (FEI): the world governing body of equestrian sport, whose rules govern any official international competition, including the Olympic Games, the Pan American Games, the World Cup and qualifying events, and the World Equestrian Games (World Championships).

Filly: a young female horse under the age of four.

Foal: a young horse still nursing from its dam.

Forehand: the part of the horse in front of the saddle, including its front legs and shoulders.

Frog: the shock-absorbing triangular growth on the underside of the horse's foot.

Gaits: the different paces at which a horse travels are the walk, trot, canter, and gallop, and varying speeds of each. There are also "gaited" horses, which are those that exhibit specialty gaits, usually lateral: the running walk, pace, and tolt are examples of such gaits.

Gallop: a fast, even, four-beat gait.

Gelding: a castrated male horse or pony.

Grazing: horses are grazing animals, designed to spend most of their time walking around in a field, cropping grass. Horses that spend as much time as possible outdoors, eating the roughage that their digestive systems require, are healthier and less prone to colic than those that spend their days in stalls and are fed twice a day.

Green: an inexperienced or unschooled horse. Term may be applied to a rider as well.

Grooming: the process of cleaning the horse's coat and hooves. Regular grooming is the rider's obligation and serves several purposes. It keeps the horse's coat healthy, stimulates the circulation, and keeps the rider in touch with the horse.

Hand: unit of measurement for horses and ponies. A hand equals four inches, and the horse is measured from the ground to the withers. A horse measuring 60 inches from ground to withers would thus be referred to as "a 15-hand" horse. A horse measuring 62 inches would be referred to as "15.2," (pronounced "fifteen two"), a horse measuring 63 inches would be "15.3," and a horse measuring 64 inches would be "16h."

Hand gallop: a brisk canter.

Headshy: a horse that jerks its head away from an approaching hand is said to be headshy.

Immunizations: twice a year horses require vaccinations to keep them safe from contracting various unpleasant and expensive diseases.

Junior: rider under the age of eighteen.

Knockdown: an obstacle is considered knocked down when a horse or rider, by contact, lowers any element that establishes the height of an obstacle. Interestingly, should the horse dislodge an element of the jump that does not lower the height of the jump, for example a middle rail, no jumping faults will be incurred.

Leads: at the canter, one front foot is ahead of the other. A horse will normally canter on the lead that matches his direction: left lead to the left, right lead to the right.

Leathers: short for stirrup leathers.

Manners: a horse's manners are partly the result of its disposition but largely the result of its training.

Mare: female horse or pony over the age of four.

Markings: the white that is present on some horses' face and legs, for example, a blaze or stocking.

Near side: the left side of the horse.

Off course: a horse is considered "off course" if it deviates from the course as outlined on the posted diagram.

Off side: the right side of the horse.

Oxer: a single fence composed of two or three parts to produce a spread, or width, effect. A "square" oxer is equal in height in both the front element of the spread and the back, making it a more difficult fence to jump.

Panic Snaps: special snaps that can be opened even when the ropes are being pulled taut by a panicking horse (hence the name). The handler can open the snaps by sliding a part of them.

Points: the colors of the mane, tail, and legs. Bay horses have black points.

Pommel: the arched front part of a saddle.

Pony: an equine 14.2h or less, unless the equine is an Arabian, in which case it will always be referred to as a horse, regardless of its actual height.

Prepurchase exam: the process of having your veterinarian check your prospective horse for health and soundness.

Rails: horizontal wooden poles used to create a jump. The upright end sections that hold the rails are called *standards*.

Refusal: a horse that avoids a jump by stopping in front of it has refused the jump; the action is called a *refusal*.

Reins: the leather straps connecting the bit to the rider's hands. Good-quality reins are an investment in safety.

Riding sneakers: sneakers with a steel shank and low heel, designed for riding. These are excellent, affordable, and comfortable, not only for young riders but for their nonriding parents.

Round: a rider's turn in each class or event, although the term is usually used only in jumping classes.

Run-out: a horse that avoids a jump by running past it to one side or the other has "run out" to avoid the jumping effort.

Salt: an essential part of every horse's daily diet, usually provided in the form of a salt block in the stall or field. Plain salt blocks are white; mineralized salt blocks are red-brown.

Schooled: a schooled horse is a trained horse, one that has been taught to understand and respond instantly to signals from the rider.

School horse: a horse used in lessons at riding schools. School horses can make wonderful first horses for children, but good school horses are rarely available for purchase.

Scope: a term used to refer to a horse's athletic ability, especially jumping ability. An exceptionally able horse would be called "scopey."

Seat: the way in which a rider sits a horse. A rider with a "good seat" is a rider with a deep, balanced position that allows the free and independent use of hands and legs.

Sire: the father of a horse.

Snaffle: a bit that works by direct pressure on the horse's mouth. A snaffle bit can have a straight or slightly curved mouthpiece or one with one, two, or more joints.

Soundness: the state of being uninjured.

Spread fence: a jumping obstacle with width. A horse must jump out as well as up to clear the fence. Also called "oxer." See *vertical.*

Stallion: male horse or pony over the age of four.

Star: a white mark on the horse's forehead, between or above its eyes.

Stride: the amount of ground the horse covers in one step is called the horse's stride. At the canter, the average single stride of the horse is twelve feet. Jumper riders will often walk the distance between obstacles on a course to determine how many strides their horses will take to cover that distance.

Tack: horse equipment used for riding and driving.

Tacked up: horse wearing the equipment for a ride or drive.

Time allowed: a specified period of time to complete a show jumping course. If the time allowed is exceeded, time faults will be added to the horse's score.

Trained: see *schooled*.

Trot: a two-beat diagonal gait; the horse's left hind and right foreleg move together, followed by a moment of suspension, then the horse's right hind and left foreleg move together.

United States Equestrian Team (USET): the organization that trains and equips equestrian teams on behalf of the American Horse Show Association (ASHA) for the United States for all major international competitions, such as the World Equestrian Games (world championships) and the Olympic Games.

United States Pony Clubs (USPC): a national organization with uniform standards for certification in horsemanship.

Vertical: a fence with no spread element. It requires the horse to make a steep arc in its effort to clear the obstacle.

Veterinarian: you will see, and pay, your veterinarian at least twice a year for routine veterinary care. You may see and pay him more often, if your horse becomes injured or ill.

Vetting (or *vet-check*): see *Prepurchase exam*.

Voluntary withdrawal: the decision by the rider not to continue on a course and to exit the ring or course, usually indicated by pulling up and tipping the hat to the judge. A rider may decide to withdraw because of a problem with the horse or trouble negotiating the course, or because the rider knows he or she has too many penalties to place in the ribbons.

Walk: the slowest, lateral, four-beat gait of the horse.

Water: an essential part of every horse's daily diet. Horses must always have access to fresh, cool water, and a healthy horse will drink ten to twelve gallons each day.

Weanling: a young horse that has been weaned (is no longer nursing from its dam).

Withers: the bony area just in front of the saddle, between the horse's back and neck. Horses are measured from the withers to the ground. See *Hand*.

Yearling: a young horse between the ages of one and two years.

Young rider: international FEI age group designation indicating riders between the ages of sixteen and twenty-one.

INDEX

INDEX

INDEX